Melanie J. Saward

Ministry Stinks

One leader's journey from despair to joy

Ark House Press
PO Box 1722, Port Orchard, WA 98366 USA
PO Box 1321, Mona Vale NSW 1660 Australia
PO Box 318 334, West Harbour, Auckland 0661 New Zealand
arkhousepress.com

© Melanie J. Saward 2019
All rights reserved. No part of this publication may be reproduced, stored in a retrieval system or transmitted in any form or by any means electronic, mechanical, photocopying, recording or otherwise without the prior written permission of the publisher.

Cataloguing in Publication Data:
Title: Ministry Stinks
ISBN: 978-0-6485780-6-2 (pbk.)
Subjects: Christian Resource;
Other Authors/Contributors: Saward, Melanie J.

Cover Design Groundcrew Agency
Layout by initiateagency.com

Contents

Acknowledgements   v
The journey to writing this book   i
My faith story   iii

Chapter 1:	There's not a lot of grace for the leader	1
Chapter 2:	Your greatest temptation	21
Chapter 3:	Pastors be talkin'	63
Chapter 4:	Meeting your capacity	89
Chapter 5:	Identity loss	129
Chapter 6:	Beware the bubble	161
Chapter 7:	You will get discouraged	175
Chapter 8:	There's never enough…	208
Chapter 9:	The enemy will attack you	227

Conclusion   256
Reference List   263

Acknowledgements

I want to acknowledge my Lord Jesus, without whom I am an utter mess and without hope. This book is my worship to you.

Secondly, my husband Josh. You've been the rock in our household, and I can't thank you enough for that. Thank you for not giving up on me when I had given up on myself.

To my wonderful daughter, Leela. You are the apple of my eye. You have always shown such compassion and grace, even as a 6 year old. I hope that when you are old enough to read this book, it might provide you with some insight into the kind of leader I have always tried to be. To you and the church.

My parents. I'm not even entirely sure whether you will ever read this. But if you do find yourself doing so, I want you to know that I have always tried my best to honour and respect you. I truly do love you and pray for you every day. You set such an incredible example to me of friendship, loyalty, respect, kindness and compassion.

Hanski, Hannah Smith, my best friend and confidante. You are a sister, not just a friend. I wish we weren't in different cities, but I love that we still are a part of each other's lives and can share life.

Pastor Dan Harding, I am so grateful for the trajectory you set me on because of your stellar example of character and skill. Thank you for just being faithful regardless of the circumstances. You are an example of kindness, wisdom and understanding to everyone who knows you.

Pastor Amanda Simmons, you are the strongest person I know. I am so grateful for every time you were there for me with my complaints, hurt and tears. I know of no one who has sacrificed more for the ministry call, and I pray that I have done you proud in my efforts to bring some perspective back for the generations of leaders to come.

Pastor Mark Dean, when I get a chance, I will make this an audiobook. But I am pretty sure it won't include the acknowledgements...so you'll just have to read this. Thank you, thank you, thank you for being such a great listening ear and wise voice in some of my hardest times.

I want to thank my entire Arrow cohort! I so regret that we didn't get that tattoo. Maybe at the reunion? Thank you for listening to my rants, and my brutal honesty. Thank you for creating such a fun and safe environment to be silly and vulnerable. Jody Destry - thank you for being such an exceptional prayer partner. And peace to my QLD peeps - Dani Bryant and Chris England, both legends! Special mention to Cath Tallack, who just makes leadership look effortless.

ACKNOWLEDGEMENTS

Pastor Murray and Jane Averill, thank you for taking a chance on me all those years ago. If it weren't for you, I wouldn't even be in ministry.

Thanks to Pastor Nathan Bean for your encouragement and support of this massive leap of faith. I really appreciate your feedback. I definitely appreciate you as a Pastor. You are a real blessing to the community.

And last but not least, my amazing editor, Elizabeth Swanson who was so gentle and wise in her suggestions. This book would have had no chance without your input. Thank you.

The journey to writing this book

About four years ago, I was approaching my first 12 months of full-time paid ministry. In that time, I had a tumultuous ride of disappointments and frustrations, with significant pockets of joy and elation. After trying to organise yet another event, I found myself confronting some very depressing thoughts. At 7am in the morning, I had dropped my two year old daughter to day care and planted myself in a prayer room at the church. I proceeded to write a list in my journal, that I titled "Why Ministry Stinks". A few days later, prompted by the Holy Spirit, I returned to the list and the prayer room. In that sitting, I was shocked to find examples in scripture where Jesus was challenged with every item I had listed and of course overcome. It was meant to be a cathartic exercise, only for me, and never to be seen by any other leader. But overtime I have come to realise that sharing verbally some of the points I wrote under that list, has proven to be helpful to others particularly those new to ministry who are:

- often navigating some unknown territory
- are unsure of what the questions are to ask to survive it
- just have no idea of what is normal

This book is a presentation of some of the points I wrote that morning, and how I came to reconcile the arduous and trying aspects of ministry that I now reflect upon with fondness and enrichment. I can put my hand on my heart and say, that I made it past the few tipping points of burnout and premature quitting, to leave my first ministry role with positivity and peace. I was blessed to have an incredible Pastor supervise me for a portion of that time, and he taught me many lessons about sustaining oneself the long haul without hating ministry. But as you know many circumstances have to be experienced to be fully understood.

My faith story

Sharing my story is not critical, yet we all want to connect. And thus, I realise that you also would prefer to have some idea of who I am before I launch into a tirade of dot points.

Even though I became a Christian at the age of seven, I grew up in a Hindu family. This was to a significant degree a result of attending a Christian school in Sydney. I didn't really attend church until I was about 15, when I kind of 'returned' to faith from feeling rather lost. Yes, it was a strange experience being the only Christian in a Hindu family. I credit it to some weird God-setup. I often felt like an outsider to the Christian world, and an outsider to the Hindu world. I certainly had to deal with aspects of life that are unusual for the average Christian. I participated in prayers, I ate blessed fruit, I even had a prayer cupboard with images and statues in my room as my parents had nowhere else to put it in the house. I did the absolute best I could to honour my parents and still do. The church that I attended at 15, was a friends church that my family trusted. A Presbyterian church in Sydney. I loved that church, and in particular the teaching. Around the age of 18 I began attending a Sydney ACC church where many of my school friends attended. I was baptised there and ended up serving in the worship team and youth leadership. My parents began to have more of a problem with my faith at that time, because I suppose the ACC church scared them. They were convinced I was brainwashed! It would have scared them even more if they knew it was all my doing. It wasn't too long after that I was a part of a committee that ran the youth group, and I took somewhat of a lead role in the Young Adults group. There was some 'ministry success' and I felt a very strong calling to ministry. I probably wanted it too much, and various doors closed to be in church ministry in Sydney. Figuring I got it all wrong I focused on my professional field of Rehabilitation Counselling. My husband Josh and I ventured up to Brisbane where my parents had moved about a year before. A fresh start seemed in order. But ultimately I wanted to be there for my parents who had various health issues. I also wanted a chance to repair the relationship, because my time volunteering at the church, in which I overcommitted and burnt out, had taken a significant toll. I had always been there for my family, as any good Indian girl does. With the exception of my time volunteering at that church in Sydney. I have the utmost respect for my parents. My Dad still remains to me, to be one of the best leaders I have ever come across. He is influential without even trying and his humility is attractive and compelling. He's always had followers, even though he never sought them. Unfortunately, my parents got pretty disillusioned about church and I wanted a chance to redeem the time.

    I came up to Brisbane and worked in various aspects of Rehabilitation Counselling including Insurance, Workplace Health and Safety, Human Resources and Occupational Rehabilitation in the contexts of the Airline Industry, Construction and Mining. They were generally large organisations and I worked in them for about ten years, before taking time off for maternity leave to have my daughter Leela. During that time on maternity leave, I committed myself to seeking God at the first sleep my daughter had for the day. I did not anticipate how such a small decision would turn my world upside down. I grew and grew and grew. I was so passionately in love with God, that I became quite dissatisfied with my working circumstances, but had no idea what to do next. I was at church one day and felt the prompting of the Holy Spirit to pay attention to an announcement being made for the Internship Program. I knew this was my next step, and so I signed up for the following year to volunteer one day a week in the church office. It was a full and incredible year, working in the Creative team at the time. About midway through that year, I once again felt that call to ministry. I realised that God had never forgotten those desperate prayers I made more than ten years ago, He just had a different plan. By the end of that year, I was being asked to come on staff working in the Creative and Connect Group Departments and I jumped at it. Around five years later, I am now taking a break from ministry to write this book and consider my next contribution to the Body of Christ.

Ministry struggles

It would be very deceptive for me to paint a pretty picture of my experience in ministry. But it's also not accurate to paint a picture that is overly negative. At some point, I will wilfully do ministry again. I do specifically love serving God in this way. So, it couldn't have been all that bad! But the last four years have also been some of the hardest years of my life. My introduction to ministry was not at all what I expected. I often felt used, overlooked, dishonoured, alone, discouraged and many other feelings that leaders generally keep secret from the average congregation member because we like to sell an image of stability, even though it's anything but. And then there were the difficulties that my brokenness created, because ministry is a greenhouse for weaknesses. So, in general I was surprised by the array of challenges, that never seemed to stop coming. Three years later I started to ask God the big questions. "God, why have you brought me here?" At times this would be accompanied by days of unexplained depression, which would be hidden from everyone around me. Only a few months later, I was completely distracted by a complete leadership upheaval that lasted four months and ended with a change of Senior Pastor and a number of staff resignations. Everything changed. The environment that I had come to know was never to be the same again. The leaders changed, my colleagues changed. I changed! I've since come to realise that such leadership troubles are a lot more common in churches than we would care to know. Thankfully at the time, I was able to keep my head above water as a result of the Arrow Emerging Leaders program[1] and the confidantes that I gained there. The Arrow program was once again God's grace and providence to carry me through a difficult time. My excitement for doing things for God, would have almost completely vaped out by the disillusionment and disappointment that followed

> **The romanticised version of ministry, will never make a leader last the test of time**

that season, were it not for my cohort and Arrow experience. Clearly I'm grateful.

I often reflect and wish that my first experience in ministry were a rosier one, selfishly so that I could keep the fantasy alive. But I've come to realise that I may not have grown as much as I did were it not for the tougher experiences. Graduating from university, I landed a job that was probably on the bottom of my list of preferences. But it was a job and it paid the bills. It was also a complete nightmare. There were so many factors that were unreasonably difficult about that workplace. But when you are in a storm, you very quickly learn how to survive, whether by anchoring yourself or learning to swim. It wasn't until I went to the next job that I realised that the first job had given me a much richer and deeper understanding of the field. It allowed me to excel beyond my peers because I had no choice but to learn everything the hard way. And the hard way is always memorable. I'm no longer naive about ministry, and I'm definitely a lot wiser. I also think I love ministry more now. Those rose-tinted glasses you wear in the first phase of ministry, actually mask a lot, including the good (surprisingly). The raw beauty of nature is preferable to a photoshopped image in a magazine. And the romanticised version of ministry, will never make a leader last the test of time. It won't make us become the leadership sages that once made more headlines, like Billy Graham, than the disgraced leaders that now make headlines. It's funny how it's often the extremes of life that develop true discernment. Just like Solomon, who tried everything under the sun to find out that true meaning is quite simple.

The goals of this book

I love the church. I often feel like I see glimpses of what God sees when He looks at His people. But just like a real marriage, its longevity relies on much more than the romance. Like anyone who loves the church, I have lamented over the disparity between the ideal that I believed God envisioned and the reality that fell painfully short. I grappled with not really being in a position to do anything really significant to bridge that gap. And through all these wrestling's - God loves His church. More than I can understand. More than you can understand. Not the building, not the preaching, not the worship...He loves His people. In His sovereignty He is able to bring justice and love into situations that I can't even bear to hear about. Even when it's awful, He still lavishes grace and love in His divinely righteous way. Even when evil forces war against, in and through the church. I have seen how God is patient, unwavering and consistent.

So, my number one goal is to open up your mind and senses to the intricate beauty and infinite messiness of the church. In a way that makes you appreciate its imperfections as yet ANOTHER cry out to the God, it so desperately needs. And to be in awe of this amazing God who perfectly orchestrates it all.

Second to this, I also want to demonstrate the incredible weightiness of being a leader in the church, that you would exercise wisdom and discernment and humility for all the days of your leadership life. Because it is a privilege to serve His royal priesthood. More precious to Him than life itself.

Thirdly, my goal is to give every new leader (whether young or old) the best chance at being able to sustain themselves for the long haul in ministry.

I ultimately share my own experiences for that reason, in hope that you might have an opportunity to learn from my mistakes and experiences in a way that enriches and lengthens your leadership journey. You will read about the hard stuff, and it will get heavy at times, but also how I've learnt to reconcile them. I walked in to ministry with an almost arrogant zeal to finally step into the call I had glorified. I was convinced that God had placed me there to do great works for the Kingdom, like the main character in some heroic quest. I was utterly surprised to discover that God's intentions were to mould me to become a different kind of leader altogether. A leader that realises that I am not at all the main character. I'm the supporting actress at best, in an epic journey, where Jesus is centre stage and hero of all. I'm more like Frodo's friend Samwise Gamgee from Lord of the Rings, who makes tea and potatoes. Our role is secondary, and we must come to embrace that if we are to have longevity. And I will do my best to help you arrive at the place that humbles yourself yet again at the feet of the only one who makes it all worthwhile.

The Jesus factor

As mentioned earlier, when I returned to the prayer room the second time I was able to observe a corresponding occasion where Jesus faced my same challenges. For that reason, a section is included at the end of each chapter titled 'The Jesus Factor' where specific situations are shared in the hopes that you too can learn from Jesus' experiences.

As believers we have the opportunity to reveal Christ in all circumstances. Leadership and ministry is yet another realm to be Christ-like. In this way, we have a unique view into the wonders of God as a gracious visionary, and appreciate Him in another

> Leadership and ministry is yet another realm to be **Christ-like**

light that maybe not everyone gets to see. We get a chance to comprehend, what it is to sacrifice, and love unconditionally, or at least attempt to. And no doubt this will draw us into an even deeper relationship with the Emmanuel, who knows all too well what leadership costs and the glorious aftermath of joy that awaits all who labour for the Father's cause.

CHAPTER 1

There's not a lot of grace for the leader

Whilst I love going out for a good meal with mates, there is one matter that I don't love so much. The split bill! Ok, so most of the time it's fine. But there are those odd occasions that a split bill seems to disadvantage me, and massively advantage everybody else. You know what I'm talking about. Those days you're not hungry, so you order soup, and everybody else orders a small animal. And then they want to split the bill evenly??!!! Why should their hunger cost me more? The whole point of the split bill is that it's even...it's fair...for everyone. And yet the dreaded split bill has failed to deliver on its purpose, time and again. I feel like 'the split bill' highlights something in us though...nobody likes that feeling of being ripped off. Nobody likes it when the scales feel imbalanced. There are areas in ministry that will feel like you are getting ripped off - but there is one that can be particularly difficult as the stakes get higher: the supposed imbalance of grace.

It was essentially my first year as a church worker, and I had been given a mammoth job. I was given the role of producing the Christmas Production, and was allocated one day a

> **There is order and priority in the Kingdom**

week to work in the Creative Department and about three days to work in the Connect Group Department. At about eight weeks out, it dawned on me the sheer magnitude of the planning and execution required to pull off the spectacular imaginative show we had designed. I counted in excess of 130 volunteers, with around 17-19 individual acts, plus managing the requests of our Senior Pastors, the volunteers and staff members. Not to mention costumes, makeup, materials, stage design, catering, rehearsals, runsheets, parking, stage movements, and of course the area that usually suffers in projects of this size: regular clear communication. I felt like the show owned my life for two months. The only way I was able to get through it, was by neglecting the components of my life that were usual features. I spent so much money eating out, because I had no extra time for preparing meals. I was reusing clothes that probably needed a wash, but I didn't have the time. My house was a literal pigsty, so nobody was allowed to come over. I was sending my daughter to day care with slightly dirty clothes (or worse yet, I would just go buy more clothes, and continue to contribute to our already escalating debt). I kept telling myself that as long as I had my family fed and my daughter showered, I was winning. My husband was amazing, he shared so much of the load at home, but he was also under his own pressures at work. I hardly slept, I was constantly out, and I neglected the other department I worked in for the entire eight weeks. There was no time for friends or family. I was working every weekend. Even on Sundays I would miss church a lot of the time. Disappearing into my office, just because it was extra time I could use.

    Anyhow, there was this one performance that had some teething problems. The performer felt that I had not made the expectations clear enough. Maybe it was true, but I certainly had done the best I could under the circumstances. However, instead of giving me benefit of the doubt or coming and talking to me directly, they went above my head to my Pastor in what appeared to be an effort to get me in trouble. My Pastor relayed the complaints, but was actually super supportive. It didn't matter though, because this time it got me. It was kind of the last straw. After having to hear so many people telling me where I was going wrong who seemed to care very little about me personally, I decided I had enough. I vented to my Pastor, but it was like it had done something in me that just couldn't be ignored anymore. It was time for another visit to our prayer room.

It just felt to me like the performer was being so self-centred. Couldn't they see what this show was doing to me? Couldn't they have cared or shown compassion instead of judgement? I wasn't a professional producer. In fact, I think I did a pretty good job considering! All I wanted was to be a Pastor, and this was the path that had been paved for me toward that end. I didn't have anyone to tell about my own frustrations with the significant number of volunteers who had been frequently letting me down. Not turning up on time or at all, whining and complaining about everything, not responding to emails/texts/Facebook messages/phone calls, not bringing the right gear, creating conflict and just generally not being considerate. Yet I just took it in my stride, and extended grace after grace after grace, regardless of how lame the excuses might have seemed…because that's what you do when you love people right?? I hadn't been adequately resourced, my home life was suffering, which nobody had even cared to ask me about. I was literally on the verge of breakdown and they were going to make this about them??

The reality is whilst you will have to extend grace continuously, it won't necessarily be reciprocated. It can feel like people can literally do whatever they want regardless of the consequences to you, but if you forget that one little thing: a judgement is made on you. You are literally doing everything you possibly can to equip them and serve them. In fact, it's really hard to remember the last time you did something for your family, or yourself. But it only takes one misinterpreted word, or misread signal and suddenly you are on their blacklist. I may be exaggerating a little bit, but I'm definitely not too far off the mark. Why can't they give you the benefit of the doubt? Why can't they just see that you are doing the absolute best you can? Why can't they see how much you're sacrificing?

Well, here's a tough truth…They probably never will. People may be able to empathise to a degree, but they will probably never understand the depths of what you or your family will sacrifice for the ministry call. Unfortunately, a lot of congregation members truly think that Pastors and Church leaders sit around having coffee and chatting all day. If only they really knew…

So somehow every leader has to reconcile this fact. When you get into ministry, you will extend way more grace than what will be extended to you. And somehow, we all need a game plan for navigating this reality. Because if you don't, the experience can change you, and not necessarily for the better.

Responses

There are ultimately three types of responses I've observed in leaders in relation to this challenge. Please note: these are just my observations. There isn't any hard and fast rule about the content that follows. Also, some of these traits may have existed before the experience and maybe this aspect of ministry has simply exacerbated it. My point in saying all of that, is that it's not a solid science. Just my observations.

Type 1: CONTROL
In this response, the primary goal is **perfection**. There is an illusion that the leader may be able to perfectly hold everything together, as long as they are able to know everything, be across everything and never switch off. If someone complains, they automatically assume that it must have been something they missed. They are often motivated by guilt and/or duty. But in general, they presume that almost everything relates to some fault in them.

The payoff is that sometimes the congregation member is being drastically unrealistic with their expectations. Instead of challenging the congregation member, this leader takes it as a sign that they need to work harder, do more or control more. I think the challenge is, that sometimes in church we act like a service provider. As in, the congregation member is a customer and we provide a service. Of course, leaders aren't in a service provider role, we are in the discipleship role. Which means that there are times when the best approach, is to address the individual because the issue is theirs…not ours. 'Customers are always right', is a terrible way to lead in church.

Type 2: WITHDRAWAL

In this response, the primary goal is **protection**. The leader has learnt the hard way that they are always going to let people down and that its entirely too brutal to have to hear how you are failing as a leader, so they withdraw emotionally. They may even prefer to see what they do as a job, a stepping stone, or just something other than a calling. It's a defensive way to manage the feelings of disappointment in oneself, and fearfully protect the self.

The payoff here is the authenticity and humility of the leader, which is impossible to compartmentalise. It's pretty hard to love people when you are emotionally distancing yourself. Which means that they also miss out on you sharing yourself with them, and who you are is one of the biggest reasons you are called to this. Not just what you are capable of doing.

The worst of all the payoffs in this type, is the fact you are only operating at a fraction of the potential. Withdrawn leaders struggle to grow, because at a distance it's likely to be someone else's fault. People need to feel you care, in order to lead them and that requires you to get up close and personal, and get vulnerable at times. Unfortunately, you are likely to get hurt in the process. But that is the manner of true resilience.

Type 3: EXIT

In this response, the primary purpose is **escape**. Not every person who walks away from their calling just 'can't handle it'. If you have walked away, I want you to know that there is no judgement here. Ministry is hard, so hard actually that maybe it needs to change how it's being done. But in this scenario, it just becomes too hard to reconcile the expectations. You become lonely, because you can't be honest. You also can't figure out how you are going to meet every need and please everybody, without completely sacrificing everything in your life. Even if there is anything left of it. You can feel completely disempowered because it feels like a lot of your choices in life have been dwindled down to only a few, quitting being one of them.

The payoff of course, is that you miss out on being able to do ministry and experience God's incredible faithfulness to you, His leader, as well as His people.

Unfortunately, the downside to all of these responses is that none of them have caused the leader to appropriately digest this rather unusual expectation. This principle is meant to do something in us. It's meant to grow us, and help us develop resilience (not hardness) so that we are equipped for the long term. It is supposed to make us more aware of God and His amazing ability to care for every one of His children. It's supposed to magnify His grace, increase our trust and reliance on Him and force us to focus on only that which we can achieve, for His glory.

Is everything in order?

Recently, I was at home cleaning our very messy house. I didn't have any plans for the day, so I was able to clean without any time pressures. I had intended to clean one room at a time. Instead I realised I had been circling the house, cleaning a little in each room as I went. I would start in our bedroom, and then I would find something there that needed to be put in the bathroom. Next thing I knew, I had started to tidy up in the bathroom and forgotten to return to the bedroom. And I continued to repeat this behaviour many times over. I felt quite silly when I realised what I was doing.

That wasn't a logical way to clean at all. Without real focus, I had just been reacting to what I saw. If I kept going in this way, and ran out of time, as often happens, I would have successfully cleaned a little everywhere, but not really cleaned well anywhere.

The busyness of ministry can be deceptive. We can be running around doing a lot of activity, but not necessarily doing the best activities. It is so easy in that environment of reactivity and meeting needs, to confuse ourselves and forget that there is order and priority in the Kingdom. While a cause isn't given, the church of Ephesus also got distracted as shown in Revelation 2:2-4.

> *"I know your deeds, your hard work and your perseverance. I know that you cannot tolerate wicked people, that you have tested those who claim to be apostles but are not, and have found them false. You have persevered and have endured hardships for my name, and have not grown weary. Yet I hold this against you: You have forsaken the love you had at first."*

Somehow, their first love had lost its place. We can't even be really sure from this passage, exactly what the first love had lost out to. The Ephesians had revelations, they had miracles, ... they must have if they had known the first love. Either way, Jesus wasn't happy that the first love wasn't first anymore. So, let's just take a moment to be sure that we aren't just aimlessly reacting, but that we have the order right too. Because sometimes our disappointment with the grace scale, is really because our first love is losing its place to the sheep....

Certainly, when I look back on my ministry journey, I was constantly choosing the sheep over the Good Shepherd. The amount of times I would set aside a 'Sabbath' that would get taken up with yet another volunteer, is embarrassing. I can only recall one occasion in which I knew it was worth it. I can recall this one time when I spent an entire day with a church member with the intention of pastorally caring for them, and they ended up giving me some really hurtful feedback. I couldn't believe what I was hearing. I had given up my precious personal time for this person, and it felt like an utter slap in the face. But it was my fault. I should never have given up my one and only day. I let ministry goals pervade my prayers and thoughts. I would constantly talk about ministry and church, to the point that with my Hindu parents I would often be struggling to think of topics to talk about. I stopped doing the activities I always enjoyed, and I often treated my family like I was passing time with them until I was back at church. Everything I read somehow related to church. All my goals somehow connected to church ministry. Yeah, I know, it wasn't healthy. I admit I was obsessed. My identity became so intertwined with my role. But long story short, I know what it's like to put the sheep above the Shepherd. And I've seen lots of leaders do the same. It's actually a little too easy to do.

Because ultimately, it feels good. It is a great feeling, to be significant. To matter in a person's life. To know I was making an impact, gave me the greatest feeling of influence and momentum... it was adrenalin. I'd almost call it power.

But it's never worth compromising your first love. Unfortunately, I don't think I realised how much I had compromised until I walked away from it all. I wish I had someone who had seen it happening, and held me accountable. But I guess some things you just have to learn the hard way. And I suppose this is an example of where you have to learn to lead yourself, because so much of this resides in the hidden places of our being where people can't see.

First and foremost, we love and serve Christ. Secondarily, we love and serve the body. I know it can be hard, because the lines get so greyed in ministry. Afterall, we demonstrate our love for Christ by how we love each other. But, somehow we must realise that there is still a distinction. At times I have told myself that I was loving our church, but looking back I was often motivated by other intentions. Duty, ambition, self-centeredness and insecurity were occasionally the driving force behind my extraneous serving. But I am forced to remind myself, that Christ is the one I ultimately serve. Which means, that I allow myself to be okay with not needing their grace, because at its core when I serve man, I am serving Christ; regardless of how disappointed they are with what they received. It's our worship to Christ, to serve regardless of what we receive. Is this not, the true heart of servanthood? Look, there is no doubt I love to please my fellow man. However, we are not really called to please, we are called to lead. Sometimes leading and pleasing converge, but when my focus is to serve Christ, I am much better equipped to let go of those times when I don't please my people and those times when leading and pleasing don't converge.

So, make especially sure that your first love is God, not the sheep.

Redirection

When my daughter was a toddler, she started to have tantrums if we didn't give her what she wanted. She's incredibly strong willed, so she could keep a tantrum going for quite some time. Oh man, it was stressful! Because you can't give kids everything they want, but she didn't understand that. Some of things she wanted, were downright dangerous. It was getting really difficult there for a time. Until my mum came along, and told me about redirection. Basically, the idea is to deliberately distract and redirect my daughter's attention away from the thing she wanted, to something else. It was pretty ridiculous how quickly my daughter forgot about the other object when given something new, particularly when she was behaving like she was going to die if she didn't have it immediately. So, in a nutshell - it worked.

Whilst we are called to be the hands and feet of Jesus, our primary role is to lead people toward Jesus. We are the ones who redirect attention away from this world, and toward Jesus. Sometimes their disappointment in us is really because they mistakenly believed that I could fulfil needs in them that only Jesus could fill. The problem is, that sometimes we forget that we are only redirectors too, and attempt to do more than we can.

There is one exception to this rule - new Christians. When discipling a new Christian, I recognise that they are a spiritual baby and at least initially I am going to be providing for them more than others. Just like a real baby.

But in general, we can't be Jesus for our people. Sometimes, their disappointment in me, is really about their disappointment with God. In that scenario, when I take responsibility for people, I am allowing them to maintain the wall that stands between them and God. And the reality is, I got into ministry, to knock walls down. I find I have to remind myself frequently, that my job is to **redirect** to Jesus, not to replace Him. Does that mean I stop working so hard in both practical and relational ways? No way. I am absolutely committed to being a vessel. But, when I know I am not enough for them, I can be assured that I have done all I can actually do.

The Rapscallions

There was a time when I screwed up pretty bad. I hurt a church members' feelings enough for them to move on. Everything was going fine, until I said something that I couldn't take back. There was nothing I could do to reconcile the relationship. There was nothing I could do to convince the person not to leave. I said sorry, so many times. It was never enough for them. I was gutted for months. I would wake up every morning, wondering when that feeling would disappear. The guilt and shame weighed heavily on my shoulders, at times I could barely lift my head.

The awesome thing about Jesus, unlike His followers, is that His grace is unending. There is no limitations on His ability to extend grace to us. Christ's grace is sufficient for us. Now be sure that you are hearing me right; if you have some major character flaws, for the sake of those you lead, address them immediately. Please don't pretend they aren't there. Get help. The judgement for seeking help, is nowhere near as bad as the judgement for falling into temptation. Some temptations will end your ministry career. There is literally nothing in this world, that is worth the compromise of your soul, not even ministry accolades.

> There is no **limitations** on His ability to extend **grace** to us

The only grace you really need, is that which Christ gives you. Encouragingly, Jesus hand-picked his disciples... and they were an absolute bunch of rapscallions. Seriously. Jesus treated Judas with love, all the while knowing that He would betray Him so blatantly for money. And of course, the classic Peter, who denies Jesus three times. Not long before that he was walking on water and calling Jesus the Messiah. And John, who had to keep reminding everyone that he was the one that Jesus loved. And yet, these were the ones on which the future of the church rested. He had grace for them. Imagine, the grace that is available for you.

Some home truths...
There are a few important factors common for every Christian leader to consider:

- **There is a higher accountability on leaders**
  More is expected of the leaders. There may be a genuine call on your life, and it's exciting and fun and purposeful, but the scriptures are clear that there is a higher accountability on leaders in the church. It's just a reality. We must all come to a place where we truly count the cost because the weight is really heavy at times. It's often the difference between what you want and what others need. It's the difference between giving grace and realising that you most likely won't receive it. It's not reliant on how you are treated. If you have been consumed by all the awesome things you are going to do in God, that's great. But please take some time to consider the cost. Because it is weighty, and for good reason. Our ability to impact and influence Jesus' precious children is high. That's for the good or bad. We actually have the ability to hurt, as well as heal. We have the ability to use, as well as to serve. We have the ability to divide, as well as to reconcile. There is

nothing more important to God than His people, so be sure you have counted the cost, and are ready to prepare His bride and not just your resume.

Besides your character, there is also the very weighty responsibility regarding teaching. Every person who dreams of being a preacher, has imagined themselves on the platform, watching the literal downloads happening in people's brains, whilst you speak epic revelations. But the responsibility to be truthful and accurate in your presentation of biblical ideas is so incredibly weighty, that it would be worth pulling back those fantasies of commanding a stage for a second...and just pause. Our reflection of God in our messages, need to be correct. We can't afford to skew HIM for the sake of a good point. This isn't to discourage you...I know some will read this and you are truly the Steven Furtick's of the future - and I am excited for you. But God's Word being preached accurately, is way more important than you being a preacher. So, count the cost. More is expected of you, and you will need to reconcile that if you are going to last in ministry. The Holy Spirit will empower you and help you every step of the way, but the accountability is still high.

- **We are ultimately leaders of love**
It seems like a strange question to ask, but what are we ultimately leading people to do? Actually, it's not really that strange but I am sure if I had all of you in a room, there would be a lot of commonality in our response. I presume words like "discipleship" and "surrender", "faith", "growth" would all

be a part of the discussion. I had this revelation a long time ago, that ultimately the best example I can be to my people is someone who loves God with all my heart, soul and mind and loves my neighbour. The call for every believer is simplified into two points:

- Deeply loving God
- Deeply loving people

When Jesus is talking about love here, He is meaning an all-encompassing love. He means a deeply committed love, that results in action. My point really is to remind us, that becoming a leader doesn't change that this is still every believer's highest priority. Which means, when I lead people, I am exemplifying that all-encompassing love to God and others. My greatest success as a leader, is if I can show them how to love better. One of the examples of love, is to extend grace. Mercifully. Even when I know that scale will be super-imbalanced. That is real love.

> My greatest **success** as a leader, is if I can **show** them how to love better

Practical tips

So, what do you do if you find yourself struggling with the onslaught of minimal grace from your people?

- **Improve your posture**
  Be aware of your **humanity**. You can only deliver that which

is humanly possible. There is actually a limit to what you can achieve. You can't really change someone. You're not supposed to carry the burdens of your people. Realise what you can do, and what God can do, and stay in your lane. In my role, I would constantly pray "this is your church God, this is your ministry. I'm just a steward. Thank you that I can be a part of it". Instead of possessing it, and wanting God to weigh in on what you are doing, make sure you have the order right. Then, forgive them. You must let it go, if you are to move on. Consider what might have been going on in their lives. Try and understand. And then forgive.

- **Be quick**

With point number one intact, the only thing to now do when you make a mistake is:

- Own it
- Be real about it
- Say sorry without justifying your own position
- Reconcile quickly
- Remind yourself, that you can only do the best you can
- Don't take responsibility for another person's inability to let go

Okay, so that last point is really important. So, you've said sorry, and you've genuinely repented. You've learnt the lesson that God wants you to learn. You are now no longer on the hook - which means if someone is struggling to forgive you, that's ultimately between them and God. It may actually be something that God wants them to grow in. Now I should say, that you should make every effort to truly reconcile before you let yourself off the hook. Reconciliation is so very important to God. Unity achieved via reconciliation is probably more important to God than you having a big church - just being real. So, make sure that when you reconcile, it is with a heart that wants to heal the situation. Ask the person - "What can I do, to make this right?" Then only do what is practical. If they say "resign". Then they are asking too much, and actually they have allowed themselves to be in a place of judgement over you. But asking this question can be very healing and fully acknowledges your desire to reconcile.

Final thoughts…

The imbalance of grace can sometimes just be an annoying occurrence. But sometimes, it comes to our attention, because deep down we think we deserve grace. WAKE UP CALL - It wouldn't be grace, if we deserved it. And the only reason we think we deserve it is because we've been keeping count. Sometimes we can look at our faith journey and ministry as an investment. Each time we do a heavenly act, we put a spiritual coin in the spiritual piggy bank. Whilst it is true that there are rewards in heaven for the faithful, we mistakenly believe we have the control over when those spiritual coins can be brought to the table for bargaining. We think "Oh hang on, that's a bit too much God, I think I need to withdraw from my spiritual piggy bank and just remind you of what I've earnt so far…"

Nothing you receive today, is because you have earnt it. It's all God's grace. If you enjoy ministry at all, be reminded that you are only doing it because God wills it. You may not have been the most faithful person. Nobody owes you - not God or man. So be careful when you start to expect something in return, like I have done too many times. Because keeping count, might indicate that love is not your only motivator for service. And it absolutely should be. We glorify God, and we imitate Him well when we serve out of love, worship and obedience - without a return on our 'investment'. This is what gives us freedom in serving. Anything else is just counterfeit. We testify to the enemy's nature when we keep count. Don't let yourself identify as a victim - you're not. God is faithful. But serve because you love Him, not because of what you might get out of it.

The Jesus factor

Consider how fickle Jesus followers were. On one hand, He was being followed and suffocated by the constant array of needs. At the end of His three years, He is being chosen by the same people to be crucified, over a well-known criminal. Where were his followers that wouldn't give Him space? Where were the people who were healed? Jesus WAS perfect, and his followers were still dissatisfied. Why would He have ever needed grace, when He made no mistakes? Well He didn't need their grace. And yeah, grace is probably not the right word in this context. How about benefit of the doubt? There was none of that. Their commitment to Him, was conditional. Jesus wasn't the Messiah they wanted, so they killed him. The crowds didn't consider whether their perception of the Messiah was inaccurate. They just sent Him to the cross. Of course, we know that this was all a part of God's master plan, but the masses at that time wouldn't have known that. They had seen what He could do, the way He taught, the way He spoke against the Pharisees. And yet they still opted for a revolutionary as their hope. We aren't alone when people fail to extend grace to us. Jesus knows and understands.

CHAPTER 2

Your greatest temptation

When I was growing up, my mum would constantly nag me about the tidiness of my room. I am a creative person, finding that I don't naturally gravitate toward organisation. I am often dreaming, exploring ideas, experimenting, drawing etc... and my room has always struggled to keep up with the pace of my creative outbursts. But boy, did my mum try to mould this trait, that irked her so much. She would frequently stick her head into my room and demand that I drop everything to tidy. I was always fascinated by mum's logic when it came to the presumed effectiveness of this tactic. I think she actually thought I would completely transform my natural inclination, if she hassled me enough.

Well, these days I am definitely a lot cleaner. I wouldn't say that I am a naturally clean person still, but I at least care that the house is clean.

Even though the logic behind nagging was unstable, there is one strange affect I didn't anticipate. Frequently, I now hear that voice in my head as an adult! It is subconscious a lot of the time, or it may be disguised in my own vernacular. But it's there! It's like the need to tidy has implanted itself in the fibres of my brain and it nags at me incessantly until it's resolved. So, I guess whilst it didn't prove effective in childhood, it has been presumably effective in contributing to my adult neuroses…ha! Not sure if that was what she was intending.

There is one thing that incessantly nags many leaders in ministry. It takes vigilance and strength to allude this tempter, and yet it will periodically knock at your door, desperately wanting to be let in. At times it will slip in undetected, effecting your every decision and behaviour. It's called pride.

And when pride does get in, it quickly seeps in looking to gain territory until you are completely saturated by its values. Trying to expel it once it has made a home, is an almost impossible task.

I have not seen a single more destructive mindset than pride. In ministry, it's like Superman's kryptonite. It will feed you and feed on you, all at the same time. Like the worst of all bacteria. It is harmful to everyone you lead including yourself, and yet so seductive. It is the single thing that has pained me more in leadership, than any other factor. Not just because of its presence before my own stumbles, but also because I have seen so many leaders gripped by this problem completely unaware. Unfortunately, there are also a multitude of church members discarded like collateral damage as a result of their prideful leaders. While the ship of the prideful goes down they are simultaneously firing shots of blame at everyone around them…because pride is stubborn and feels a lot better than admitting defeat.

If there was one thing I would hope that every leader would walk away with from reading this book, it would be to resolve that you will reject pride at every turn. If I had my way, there would be less books on church growth strategies, and more on conquering pride. But evidently it's not the most popular topic - but having the knowledge and wisdom to navigate pride, is probably worth more than an extra two thousand tithe paying Christians at your church this coming Sunday.

Do you see what I see?

That first six months of ministry, were a total whirlwind. I felt invincible. I feel sorry for my Creative Pastor looking back. She would probably tell me it wasn't so bad, but I know what I felt in my heart. I thought I was the answer to that team. That they couldn't do without me. I was zealous and got many projects done, but I was so full of myself. I was constantly complaining about other people in the team, and deep down I knew it was because I thought I could do a better job than them. Oh, and don't get me started on my ambitions! I was certain I was the female Brian Houston, and everybody was just standing in my way, failing to discover the innate talent and the many ways I could turn this church around. I am slightly exaggerating, but not by much. At about six to eight months in, I was finally pushed off my high horse. As always, in retrospect, there is only one word that could describe my previous behaviour: pride. I had no idea! I didn't even really necessarily think it was a problem at the time, it was so imperceptible. A friend of mine recently described to me that pride blinds you. What a perfect description. I was so unable to see how destructive my behaviours were. Gossip, judgement, harshness, impatience, selfish ambition...these were all by-products of the pride that I had adopted and chosen to be my lens for six months. I was the problem.

In my observations, when we talk about character in the

leadership context, generally we talk about the really overt and obvious. Sexual temptation. Lack of Integrity. Pride tends to take a back seat. I've never heard it talked about at a conference and I don't think I've even heard it preached about from a pulpit. But pride is talked about so much in scripture and there is a particular susceptibility to it when you're a leader. There definitely appears to be a strong relationship between power and pride. Pride is one of the enemies most well used and effective tools. It's arguable that some of these falls from grace have their origins in pride.

The further I went in leadership, the more I discovered the layers of my own pride and I continue to do so today. As I continued to repent and humble myself, God opened my eyes to more than I could have imagined.

What is pride?

In a nutshell, being proud is the opposite of humility. In my observations, and through searching scriptures, there appears to be two modes of operation for pride. There is the pride in relation to others, and the pride in relation to God:

- **To others**

    Pride in this mode pertains to how you see yourself as better or more significant than others. It basically believes that you are more valuable than those around you, and you in turn will treat people as lesser than yourself. Whilst love seeks to benefit others, and to elevate those it serves, pride seeks to benefit the self and elevate the self. In ministry, it's likened to the scriptural statement "shepherds who feed only themselves" (Jude 1:12). Pride leads to unloving behaviours, or establishes relationships that benefit the leader...which is arguably not love at all.

It is important to state here, that the area which testifies to the humility or pride of a leader is how they treat their own leaders both staff and volunteers. Most would presume that the staff and key volunteers would be the best off for being under a strong loving leader. And don't get me wrong many church staff members are very cared for and loved. I am still praying that I get a call from Pastor Craig Groeschel one day to be a part of his staff. But unfortunately, a proportion are not. It is quite strange. Afterall, your most loyal followers should be treated the best. They are also your most influential. But instead there is a strange disconnect between how some leaders view their employees and their church members. It's as though love, care, support, and grace are all reserved for church members. Staff are demanded of, dishonoured, and berated etc. True, it's not everywhere... but it should be nowhere in the church. Carey Nieuwhof speaks about this workplace culture in an article he wrote about trends for 2019. In the article "5 Disruptive Church Trends That Will Rule 2019"[2], he says:

"Too many church leaders who lead people in the name of God create a team culture that feels nothing like the Kingdom of God—arrogant leadership, selfish manipulation, office politics, gossip and deceptive manoeuvring have killed far more cultures and harmed more people than you can count. All of this has left a body count of people who say they're not done with God, but they're done with church...Don't believe the cynics. This is not every Christian workplace. But it is some. And some is too many."

God doesn't make any distinctions between staff members and church members. They are all brothers and sisters in Christ, and they are all ultimately sheep. If you've left a church staff or team because you were hurt by such a leader, I am sincerely saddened that you had to go through that. That was never Gods plan, and it was actually disobedience on the part of your leader. Please see a counsellor about it, so that you may heal because the Body of Christ is still beautiful and still in need of hands to be hands, and feet to be feet. For all the facts that are being written about the millennial generation...I sincerely hope that they will eradicate this 'leadership style' and make it as obsolete as the projector, or the PowerPoint sermon...

Would our churches have the best workplace cultures in the modern world. Would the church be considered the number one place to work, instead of Google and Facebook. Love is the hallmark of the Christian faith. And love should be the hallmark of every church office and leadership meeting. Leaders: don't lead them, if you can't love them. I love the words in Proverbs 3:27

> *"Do not withhold good from those to whom it is due, when it is in your power to act."*

Do good to your staff and volunteers.

☐ To God

With regard to God, pride is demonstrated in believing that we don't need God. The average Pastor would refuse the notion that they might not believe they need God. That's a trait we usually reserve for a non-believer. But as always behaviour is much more honest. Anyone can say anything. We must recognise that the ultimate goal is to lead as He desires. To even begin to think that as leaders we may not need God, would seem ludicrous. But it happens, and here are just some ways you can tell:

- We stop asking God what He wants (Psalm 10:4)
- We stop praying
- We copy other churches

Of course, that last point is not really always a problem. Sometimes it is good to follow the way of another church. It is included because it can become another symptom of not relying on God to do the part only He can do. Even if you have a relationship with God, where you can't hear Him or you can't always see what He wants, that's okay. The onus is on us to ask God, regardless of how He responds. Asking Him recognises the authority He has over the church.

There are obviously more personal symptoms of a non-reliant relationship with God. Maybe you've stopped praying altogether. Maybe you've stopped seeking Him. None of us are perfect at this. But, we know when it has become a real problem.

A non-reliant relationship with God is also characterised by sin and rebellion. It's interesting how we can be a leader in a church, and be the furthest from Him. It's because religion, doesn't require intimacy to sustain itself.

Depicting a very genuine posture of humility and reliance by the King at the time, 2 Chronicles 14:11 is a favoured example of the humility of leadership before God:

> *"Then Asa called to the Lord his God and said, "Lord, there is no one like you to help the powerless against the mighty. Help us, Lord our God, for we rely on you, and in your name we have come against this vast army. Lord, you are our God; do not let mere mortals prevail against you."*

The language is so humbling. Asa cries out to God, recognising the significance of the part God has played in any military success. They rely on Him. When is the last time you have relied on God? We are so foolish to think that we are the greater proportion in the God-Us duo. He is often making the circumstances right, sending the right people, softening hearts, bringing revelation, and so many other components before we even step into the room. If we were to really grill down and ascertain a percentage on the proportion of contribution, it would be something like 80% God, to 20% us. That's not even considering the fact that He has literally made you, with your unique personality and traits, given you the spiritual gift. Yes, that's right. He gave you the gifts for teaching, prophecy and shepherding. It wasn't earned or your right. He gave you the set of circumstances that find you where you are, and put you at the right place at the right time…so yeah, the percentage is probably more like 95% God, to 5% us when you factor all of that in. We simply are way more reliant on Him than we can even imagine. Pride comes into play when you fail to acknowledge that.

> **We simply are way more reliant on Him than we can even imagine**

The most important factor

If all the points I tell you in this chapter are not enough to convince you, then this is the one point you need to know...

God doesn't like pride.

Okay, that's it. The chapter is finished. Mic dropped. We shouldn't need any greater reason than this. Proverbs 3:34 says

> *"He mocks proud mockers, but shows favour to the humble and oppressed".*

This scripture is iterated again in 1 Peter 5:5 where Peter is encouraging all to be clothed with humility toward each other -

> *"God opposes the proud, but shows favour to the humble"*

Our whole faith journey is about pleasing God. So, pride should be left behind.

Not that you would need more motivation after that first staggering point, but scripture also tells us that pride:

☐ **Guarantees mistakes**
Proverbs 16:18 *Pride goes before destruction, a haughty spirit before a fall.*

☐ **Creates arguments & conflict**
Proverbs 13:10 *Where there is strife, there is pride, but wisdom is found in those who take advice.*

- **Will embarrass you**
  Proverbs 11:2 When pride comes, then comes disgrace, but with humility comes wisdom.

- **Makes you selfish**
  Phil 2:3 *Do nothing out of selfish ambition or vain conceit. Rather, in humility value others above yourselves.*

- **Skews the vision**
  I haven't got a direct verse for this, but I've seen it enough to know that pride definitely gets in the way of the purpose and mission. It might be as subtle as believing that your goal is to be a good preacher, instead of making disciples (often notice how pastors will hassle their congregation members to save the lost, but make no effort personally to do that? And yet modelling is the most effective form of leadership).

On the other hand, the humble attract the following according to scripture:

- **The Leading & Teaching from God**
  Psalm 25:9 *He guides the humble in what is right and teaches them his way.*

- **God's sustenance**
  Psalm 147:6 *The Lord sustains the humble but casts the wicked to the ground.*

- **God's favour and success**
  Psalm 149:4 *For the Lord takes delight in his people; he crowns the humble with victory.*
- **God honours you**
  Proverbs 15:33 *Wisdom's instruction is to fear the Lord, and humility comes before honour.*

Being humble, isn't just an attitude. It's also obedience. It means that you will relinquish your rights, and rather follow God even if it doesn't make sense. I myself am in a place of anonymity right now. I left my role as a Pastor, with only my provisional accreditation and have no idea if I'll be able to keep it. But I knew that God wanted me to move on. I have had fears about my future in ministry and wondered why God did all He did, the way he did. Believe me, I have wrestled a lot in the quiet place. I have chosen to take the path of humility wherever that leads me, because I want to obey God even if it doesn't make sense. I trust Him and His Word.

Some behaviours

The heart is deceitful above all things. We don't understand it, especially our own heart. Which is why asking yourself if you are proud is one of the least effective ways of really knowing. Here are some of the most obvious signs of pride.

- **You're preoccupied with image over reality**
  Another way of putting this, is that you are more concerned about how things appear than how they actually are.

Are you often worried about how things look? There were many times that I stuffed up in leadership, and there will be many more. But I know that only God has the right to judge me. So, take ownership for how things look. People are going to judge you even when things look good. Why let opinion be your guide? At least nobody can deny that you are transparent, honest and authentic. When I am conscious of how I might look or people's judgements, I make a concerted effort to not change their minds. When you find out that someone doesn't really like you, or they have misunderstood a circumstance involving you…you may be tempted to change the situation. Maybe you work extra hard to get on their good side, and show them that you are actually really likeable. You try to talk to them and change their mind. Or maybe you go the opposite route and discredit them? Well…what I try to do is, and I've been getting a lot stronger…I do nothing. I let them think lowly of me even if it hurts or bugs me. I don't work any harder, and I don't let it change my view of them. The more I do this, the less I will take responsibility for the ways people might judge me. And the stronger I'll get at being rejected. Because God knows I've got more rejection coming my way, in leadership. It is humbling to take ownership for how something looks. It's healthy for your leadership. So, the five people who left your church recently because of closing a ministry arm…just own it. You probably knew it might happen anyway. Leaders take ownership, sometimes even when they don't need to. Nehemiah is a classic example. In Chapter 1, Nehemiah says this epic prayer, where He confesses the sins of the Israelites. He probably didn't have the 'authority' to do that, but He did it anyway. He took ownership and responsibility for His people. It's no surprise to me that God honours Him, by allowing Him to be the one who leads change. The only person who worries about how things appear, is probably more than likely a person who is ruled by inadequacy and the approval of man. These are voices we are meant to silence and put to death when becoming a self-sacrificing leader.

- **You judge harshly and quickly**
  If you really struggle to give people a second chance, then you should probably take a look at your pride levels. Our faith is all about second chances. Closing the door forever on a person, is a completely prideful act. It makes the assumption that you have never needed a second chance. People aren't actually there to please you anyway. If you make grandiose judgements and are quickly critical about others, you have become lost in the machine of the church and misunderstood your position.

- **You can't apologise**
  Apologising is an interesting one. Leaders often won't apologise because they believe it shows them as weak. We wouldn't have to protect our reputations if we trusted that God will give us favour with man when we need it. Maybe in a general leadership setting this should be a concern, although many leadership gurus suggest authenticity and humility also very relevant to the business world. In church leadership, I would argue that this is very backward logic. We are meant to confess our sins, we are meant to reconcile. In fact, these are the very areas of faith we should be trying to take the lead on. I'm not talking about publicly every Sunday, but to

those we have hurt. Apologising doesn't always mean that you are saying you are at absolute fault for everything, it's sometimes an acknowledgement of hurt and a desire to heal and move forward. The wonderful Pastor Dan Harding was one of the humblest people in this regard. He gave such an incredible example for me. He was always quick to reconcile and apologise. Even with me, his underling. I am always encouraged to follow in His footsteps. Relationship is more important than how I am perceived. We are also encouraged that the poor in spirit and the weak will be blessed. I can't think of a more humble quality than to apologise. It is the most obvious method to communicate when responsibility is being taken for actions.

And let's not forget what the scriptures tell us. In Matthew 5:23-24:

> *"So, if you are offering your gift at the altar and there remember that your brother has something against you, leave your gift there before the altar and go. First be reconciled to your brother, and then come and offer your gift."*

Okay, so it may not be so direct to say apologise, but it does suggest that we do whatever we can to reconcile with our brothers before we come to the altar.

- **You are unhealthily driven**
  It's fairly normal to be driven. At times it can be something that God has actually put on your heart. A burden or a yearning to see something that He has birthed in your heart and spirit.

But, as with all things, there is a line that gets crossed when it becomes unhealthy. How do I define an unhealthy drive? In a general sense, when it becomes selfish ambition or idolatry. The best book I could recommend, because honestly I don't think I could do a better job by talking about this subject... is Counterfeit Gods[3] by Tim Keller. Insightfully, he gets into greater detail about success as an idol. Sometimes church can become our idol, making us no different to the workaholics of the business world. We start to sacrifice people, relationships and character on the altar of church growth. Common things I've seen sacrificed are:

- **Love for all people**
  Paul talks so much about how we as believers are to treat each other. Submissive, patience, kindness, unity, respect are just some of the words he uses to describe the nature of our interactions with each other. Unfortunately, all too often I have seen church leaders and pastors more concerned about their progress that they devalue the sheep. God is way more interested in how we are treating each other than whether we had enough people turn up to an event. It doesn't have to be an either-or situation, but sometimes we make it that way. The best sign is how you treat those individuals that aren't cool, or aren't popular. When you are unhealthily driven you'll care more about the ones who can do something for you.

- **Your family/marriage/friendships**
  Sometimes we can sacrifice our families for the sake of

ministry. Our identity can become so invested in ministry, that we forget about them. I talk about this in more detail in chapter 5 & 6.

- **Your health & hobbies**
When you start to neglect yourself and your own personal interests, it can be really detrimental.

- **Your time with God and the health of that relationship**
Your relationship with God, becomes a performance or exclusively an equipping for your calling. As in you've become business associates as opposed to a father and child.

- **Rest and personal time**
Who has time for rest? There is so much to do, right? If you think that way, it's not a good sign. I've heard of leaders say "Live while I'm alive and sleep while I am dead" as a justification for their overactivity. That's not biblical. Jesus rested, ate and had time to himself often. Don't deceive yourself, it's a sign of being unhealthily driven.

- **Your original desires for getting into ministry**
Sometimes I've seen leaders who have gotten into ministry because they want to serve. As time progresses, their only concern becomes the platform or whatever else looks important and not for the right reasons. This is certainly a sign of idolatry. 'Ministry' has become more important than the reason you began it in the first place.

I recently watched the movie *Founder*[4], the story of Ray

Kroc who turned the McDonald's business into an empire. I'm not sure how accurate the story is, but I love the analogy that the writers gave. At the beginning, Ray was so intoxicated with the dream of franchising this exceptional business. He was willing to put so much on the line, because the vision of such a restaurant being accessible for the average American had gripped him. He was passionate about the food industry, and he was passionate about McDonalds. Somewhere along the line though, he turned into this greedy businessman who cared very little about the thriving hospitality industry that once inspired him. It can be like that with ministry too. We start out with the intention of discipling people. Before you know, ministry accolades are our focal point.

- **You've stopped trying to learn and grow**
Every church leader desiring to grow their church will read the latest church strategy book myself included. Or they will read copious amounts of theological literature to improve their preaching. This isn't the type of learning and growing I am talking about. I am talking about in the inner-man or inner-woman. We often talk to our congregations about transformation, not realising that we are also supposed to be engaged in an ongoing process of transformation. If we are truly disciples, we will live with more freedom, more peace and more joy than the year before. Of course, such growth is not so linear, but you get my point. The one area which should be a given, is that our love for God and people should be richer, more submitted, more understanding, more patient, more selfless, more consuming than it was before. You want to see

your church members grow? Why not model the journey of a true disciple. Show them that you are committed to growing more in love with God, and people.

☐ **You think your church can't do without you**
When you recognise that you are a co-shepherd, you understand how untrue this statement is. We are all special to God, but we are all replaceable as leaders. We should be moving out of the way for the next generation. This should force us to consider the leaders to be developed and how we can empower them. There's a significant line in the book of Esther, and no it's not the one you are thinking of. The one you are thinking of is:

> *"...Who knows but that you have come to your royal position for such a time as this?" Esther 4:14*

The one I'm referring to is very close by:

> *"For if you remain silent at this time, relief and deliverance for the Jews will arise from another place".*

Mordecai was so confident in God's faithfulness to His people that he knew everything wasn't riding on Esther. God is faithful to His church. Jesus said He will build it. If you aren't there, He will raise up someone else. God's plans are not resting on you alone. Hopefully that also makes you relax a bit.

☐ **Your mind can't be changed**
There are times when we make the wrong call about something. It's normal. We misconstrue situations, our own prejudices

influence our perception, our strategy didn't work. There isn't a single person who can't relate to that. But, if you make a bad call but can't own up to it and have your mind changed? That's pride. I recently watched the documentary on Netflix about the Fyre Festival[5]. This was going to be the most epic luxury music festival of all time. What a visionary Billy McFarland appeared to be?! Instead the whole project slowly crashed and burned, along with Billy's dignity. It left function goers without millions of dollars...It is quite interesting to watch, in terms of how the whole event planning started to deteriorate. One fact stood out about the behaviour of Billy McFarland. Whilst so many of his staff members and contractors repeatedly told him of risks and issues, and even straight out told him to cancel the whole event...He would not change his mind. What is that? What was he waiting for? Pride. It's possible there were other factors at stake: fear, inexperience. Either way, not being able to change your mind is not necessarily a sign of good leadership, it can just be arrogance. There is a reason that King Solomon and other contributors to Proverbs often write about sage advisors being a blessing to a King. If you believe you have solid people around you, then you should listen to them. That's right make sure you have the kind of people who are trustworthy and willing to speak up when you are doing something stupid. If they say that it's time to change direction, for the sake of developing humility, listen to them with an open mind.

☐ **Your response to hurt is vengeful or entitled**
Everybody gets hurt in ministry. If I'm being really honest, the

higher you go the more potential you have to be hurt. Maybe it's someone you invested time in that leaves the church. Maybe it's just how brashly someone spoke to you. Maybe it's the tons of criticism that you get. There are plenty of circumstances to get upset by. If you want to grow into a strong leader, it's beneficial to pay attention to your gut response when you get hurt. But of those responses, there are two responses that can certainly point to the presence of pride. Vengeance and entitlement. If you have been badly hurt and you are wishing that something bad would happen to that person or the more palatable version "God will teach them", there's a good chance that pride sits under the surface. Don't worry, this isn't to condemn you. My advice would be to get to a counsellor and bring those raw emotions out in a safe place, so that they can work through it with you. Don't deny they exist - that won't change anything. Vengeance has this undertone that mimics a set of scales that need to be balanced. Vengeful people will make comments like "I'm going to get even". The reason vengeance can be rooted in pride is because it assumes that it's impossible for you to have harmed someone. Which is just a lie. Half the time, we may have no idea how often we hurt people. People don't always tell you. Even the nicest people in the world can say something that harms another.

    Entitlement is that voice that says, "How dare they?", "Do they know who I am?", "They have no right to do that". "No right" is the biggest giveaway statement pointing to entitlement. It suggests that there is something about you that should preclude you from pain. That you believe you don't deserve it, or that somehow pain or negative behaviour should not be given to someone as good as you are. None of us actually want pain, but it is as guaranteed as the sun rising in the morning. The enemy doesn't play fair, so expect unfair treatment. But don't miss the opportunity to allow it to do a work in you, to make you a stronger, freer and more humble leader.

- **You are trying to change people**
Sometimes we can disguise our desires to change people as caring. And to some degree it's not always wrong. If we see someone in a harmful situation, we aren't wrong to want to set them free. I think where pride comes in, is when we assume that we know the answers to a person's situation and force our advice onto them. Firstly, you don't even know if someone wants your advice. Maybe you aren't exactly the person they want to be like. Maybe they can see something in you that you don't see. If there is anything I know, it's that people don't necessarily follow their own advice. For that reason, I often ask if someone wants my advice before I say anything. And if they do, I will always preface it with 'you can take it or leave it'...'you don't have to do what I say, I could be wrong'. In a lot of cases, I will even prefer not to directly answer a request for advice and rather present the various options and possible outcomes of each situation. Then it's up to them to decide.

My assumption being that maybe they can't see the full scope of the situation clearly, and once they get that clarity they'll feel capable of deciding for themselves. Ultimately, I do that because I believe they have the Holy Spirit in them, and I'm just there to help them hear the Holy Spirit clearer. What I've come to realise is that my guidance is highly opinionated and influenced by my own cultural experiences, expectations and values, that aren't necessarily uniquely Christian. Secondly, no matter what I say to a person, it is the Holy Spirit that can truly change a heart. Believe me, I have tried to change others and ultimately I discover time and again, that some things aren't meant to change. It's just my self-righteous pride that thinks they do. My job is to teach God's principles regardless of whether they take it on. I shudder to think about the times I have heard some of the most strenuous life situations, where some well-meaning Christian has tried to come in and give a one liner from a sermon they heard. Just like Job's friends, who tried to come in and 'figure out' why God was punishing him. We would be wiser to admit that sometimes we genuinely don't know why certain things happen, and that none of our advice is ultimately going to change a person's predicament. Promise to be there for people instead.

- **You think everyone should be like you**
 This is by far the most annoying one. I am a pretty vulnerable person, and at times have aired my frustrations with ministry to a fellow Pastor. I find that they think my desire to vent is an opportunity for them to tell me how I should be more like them. As though there is only one way to lead. I know I'm being a bit nasty...I just find pride annoying like most of us. I have always tried in my leadership to ensure that I value difference. That I recognise that my church doesn't need more me's. It is the height of arrogance to think that I am the standard and that everyone should conform to my image. I have termed

this concept: Spiritual Superiority. My definition of Spiritual Superiority is this idea that we leaders concoct, that suggests that the reason God put me in my role is because I am actually superior to the people I lead. Which means, I'm the preferred model of Christianity. Maybe I am in the role because I am just good at certain tasks that God is wanting to see in my church, at that time. Maybe it's just because He has called me to it. Don't even get me started on this whole concept of being called...can any of us really say why we have been called? There are plenty of faithful people in the Kingdom, it didn't have to be me that was specifically called to ministry. Sometimes we just need to tone the 'I am special' language down a bit. Yeah we are special, but not because we have done anything that warrants that. We are special because we are His.

☐ **You control others**
Control is the desire to withdraw a person's freedom. To restrict. Control is the enemy's hate-language. Do you like what I did there? Instead of love-language, I said hate-language...I'm so clever...The enemy parades control as freedom. God operates in the realm of freedom, in that he gives us free will even if our choices ultimately hurt Him or lead to our demise. Controlling people use fear, shame, guilt, and the weaknesses of others to get submission. Sounds pretty unhealthy to me. Unfortunately, the church has a sordid history with believers using such behaviours to demand submission. Especially leaders. So, be aware; are you using fear to get your employees to do what you ask? Maybe the

fear of termination or isolation? Are you saying cruel words, raising your voice, or withholding certain privileges? Are you dangling carrots over their heads that you are not delivering on? Are you slandering others to elevate yourself? Are you spreading rumours? It all stems from a desire to restrict. I've observed or heard all of these done by various leaders in the church, so don't tell yourself it doesn't happen. How you treat people matters to God big time.

In the extreme of this behaviour, you find cults. Cult leaders don't start off as cult leaders, but they certainly get absolutely delusional. I have a friend who was part of a religious cult, and boy cult leaders are messed up. We in the church should be trying to preserve freedom in its truest form in our relationships, and run like the wind away from anything that looks like control, in case we start to believe our own delusions.

The last point I want to share, is so important that it is separate from the dot points above. If you ever think that you are justified in creating disunity and division in the Body of Christ or hurting His precious children for your own gain, you have completely lost sight of God, replacing Him with a vision of yourself. There is nothing more important to God than unity. Causing division for your own selfish gain, is the greatest sign of pride. Whilst Martin Luther caused disunity in the Reformation era, it was for a very important reason. The true and pure message of the gospel had been clouded by power and tradition. I would suspect that

> Love and oneness are the **hallmarks** of the Christian faith

there will only be a few Christians in the history of the planet who could have been justified for such actions. But if you cause a painful church split because you just think you could do a better job, you've lost perspective of what is truly important to God. Love and oneness are the hallmarks of the Christian faith, not disunity and division. Unity is hard work. But there is nothing more loving than submitting to one another for the sake of unity. I believe God commands a blessing for that.

Pride and power

I always had this suspicion that there was a relationship between pride and power. It potentially seems like common sense, but obviously not every person who has pride has power, and vice versa. It wasn't until I stumbled across the story of Uzziah that I could see that my hunch was right.

The story of King Uzziah is found in 2 Chronicles 26:11-16.

> *"Uzziah had an army of well-trained warriors, ready to march into battle, unit by unit. This army had been mustered and organized by Jeiel, the secretary of the army, and his assistant, Maaseiah. They were under the direction of Hananiah, one of the king's officials. These regiments of mighty warriors were commanded by 2,600 clan leaders. The army consisted of 307,500 men, all elite troops. They were prepared to assist the king against any enemy.*
>
> *Uzziah provided the entire army with shields, spears,*

> *helmets, coats of mail, bows, and sling stones. And he built structures on the walls of Jerusalem, designed by experts to protect those who shot arrows and hurled large stones from the towers and the corners of the wall. His fame spread far and wide, for the Lord gave him marvellous help, and he became very powerful.*
>
> *But when he had become powerful, he also became proud, which led to his downfall. (NLT)*

It was at the very moment of becoming powerful, that pride emerged. In the case of King Uzziah, the relationship was strong. It makes sense right? Power is an interesting concept. There is something about it that makes us feel indestructible, even if that power is given by God. We often want the authority, but can we really handle the power that comes with it? Can we still have good character, treat people well, and remain reliant on God when we are being given keys to the Kingdom? Of course, it's possible. A friend recently posted on Facebook an excerpt from a Francis Schaeffer interview, in which he suggests that it is much better for Christian leaders to live in absolute anonymity than to contend with power when you are unable to handle it. It's a startling reality that we prepare ourselves well for so many aspects of ministry, but we don't prepare ourselves for humility in the face of great power.

If there is anyone we have power over, it's our children. My daughter loves and trusts me implicitly. There are so many ways in which I observe how freely she trusts me. She gets upset when I am hurt. She is quick to say sorry, which the stubborn little thing does with nobody else. There is an intimacy and oneness I have with her, that is beautiful. There has never been a doubt in her mind to restrict my influence over her. She gives me total access to influence her, as I please. It's a little scary to put it that way. But it is because I love her, more than myself, that I never take that for granted. I use that power to serve her. That is why we must take care with those who put their trust in us. When someone trusts us, they are saying:

> "I give you access to my HEART..."
> "I allow you to influence me..."
> "I am surrendering and submitting myself to your leading..."
> "I am allowing myself to be vulnerable and open to your harm or good".

Trust is a precious exchange. Anything that seeks to manipulate or negate that, is simply dangerous. And we aren't dealing in the business of physical structures or anything that could be unharmed by our abuse of that trust...we deal in the ministry of hearts. There's a reason why vulnerability is hard and of great risk to humans. Vulnerability is one door that can lead to pain or intimacy. That's right, it's the same doorway, with two different paths. If trust is broken, the door can remain forever closed as a protection from pain. Unfortunately, outcomes like this also mean the door to intimacy is closed forever.

> **Vulnerability is one door that can lead to pain or intimacy**

This relationship between power and pride, is the reason I coined this term 'Stewardship of Power'. Stewardship isn't new, it just tends to be used in terms of money and other areas we believe have been entrusted to us. As leaders, there is no greater responsibility that could be entrusted to us than the very sheep the Shepherd died for.

That's why, understanding how to manage the power we are given, is of paramount importance. So how do you steward power? To be honest, I am still growing in this area. But I will share with you a few things I have learnt about responsible stewarding of power. Before I do, I just want to share one more story found in scripture.

Inadequacy and pride

The truth is, anyone can fall into the sin of pride. It's partly attractive because of the condition of the human heart which at its core desires self-glorification and self-worship. But, there is one quality that seems to make a person particularly susceptible. Inadequacy. All of us have a certain degree of inadequacy. But there is a specific quality to its nature that I will describe through a scriptural example.

King Saul is certainly a memorable character in scriptures. He is not at all the leader we would aspire to be like, but his life provides a warning. Whilst he starts out as a King with incredible inadequacies, he becomes a King full of pride. There are certainly hints of fear and rejection in his choices also, which at times make you empathise with the guy. But there is pride there too, and we can learn from him.

In 1 Samuel 9, Saul first comes on the scene. He is visiting the land in which Samuel resides and Saul is about to approach him when Samuel gets a download from God. God identifies him as the man that will rule the people of Israel. There is nothing in what God says that suggests doubt or ruin on the part of Saul. He communicates that Saul has been provided as a merciful response to the cries of the Israelite people. God clearly has confidence in Saul. However, when Samuel begins to communicate Saul's calling as the ruler over the Israelites (V20), we observe this strange response from Saul. Samuel simply states that Saul's family will be the focus of all Israel's hopes. From what I read, and I've tried a few different versions, Saul's response appears to be one of disbelief and ultimately disqualification. In one translation, Saul's response is *"Why do you say such a thing to me?"*(V21) That's the first taste of Saul's underlying inadequacy. If we pick up the story again in 1 Samuel 10:9, we see that God changes Saul's heart. We don't really see in what way God changes him, but we can see that God is equipping him for the task of kingship and that ultimately God approves of Saul. On the way back home, everything happens as Samuel prophesied. In verse 10, the Spirit of God comes powerfully upon him, and he begins to prophecy with the other prophets. However, when he returns to his uncle, he explains that he has seen Samuel, but doesn't mention being anointed as king...???!!! Strange right? Once again it's not really clear why he does this, considering the uncle is going to find out soon enough. But the writer makes a point to mention this. It's possibly another sign of his inadequacy.

But the final blow that I think verifies for me this theory of Saul's inadequacy, is the fact that all his tribe were being gathered together for the announcement of the new king...and Saul was not there. He was literally hiding in the supplies. God himself had to tell Samuel, so that they could fetch him. What was going through his head?? This is such an extreme reaction. I recall when my new Senior Pastor was presented, prayed over and anointed for the role...I can't even begin to imagine what would have happened if he didn't turn up. Or worse yet...was hiding in the church somewhere. It's not really wise to speculate, but at the very least we can see that in spite of the spirit of God coming upon him, prophesying under the influence of the Spirit, having God change his heart...all of this didn't change his inadequacy. There appeared to be something in him that just didn't believe he was the right choice. From what I read, it looks like he had truly disqualified himself. Saul was acting in every way like a person who didn't believe he was meant to be there.

All of us, at times, feel like we aren't enough for the role of leading God's people. That's not new. Even Solomon felt that. But our weaknesses and failings are not necessarily a disqualification as a leader. In fact, an important maturing process for leadership is being able to reconcile your weaknesses, and lead in spite of them. However, it is important to note here that if you fall in this category...if you feel like God made the wrong decision and it's only a matter of time before everyone else finds out? It is never too late to own that. Get yourself some help. Get understanding about why you feel disqualified, and dig deep to resolve it. God is never wrong, He is perfectly righteous in every way. Which means, you're wrong - you are meant to be where you are. Three issues are at the heart of disqualification:

- **Comparison**
  You would only disqualify yourself if the image you are painting of a leader is one you can't identify with. That doesn't mean you are the wrong person, it means the image you have may be wrong. The images we have of leadership are developed

through the leaders we've observed, people we like, and even our parents. They aren't necessarily drawn from scripture and God's expectations of leaders.

☐ **Limited understanding of the Spirit**
If you even think that this whole responsibility of leadership is reliant on you, then you've got it all wrong. We are co-labourers. I'd say your perspective of the Spirit's capability, might need to get a lot bigger than your perspective of your capability. Get your eyes off yourself, and get them back onto God. He will build His church, remember?

☐ **You've never felt good enough**
Maybe there is something in you that has had a permanent belief that you are not good enough. Well, I hate to say it, but nothing will ever be good enough for you. Your budget will never be high enough, your building will never be big enough, your staff will never be charismatic or effective enough, your church will never be large enough. Because ultimately nothing will ever be enough to change what you feel inside. And worse yet, it's not healthy to look to those extrinsic values to validate you when those you lead are at stake. What is faulty internally, can never be fixed externally. I could write a whole book on this issue, but the best advice I could give you is to pursue healing. For myself, reading 'Exposing the Rejection Mindset" by Mark Dejesus was a game changer. My own 'not good enough' belief was stemming from lots of rejection that I had not dealt with. Every accolade was driven by my desire to prove myself wrong.

It is also really pertinent to demonstrate how Saul moved into pride, so that you can see the relationship between the two. Unfortunately, it's not too far into the story before we see a very sudden change in Saul's trajectory. Saul was told to wait seven days for Samuel to arrive and offer the burnt offerings and sacrifices (1 Samuel 13). Whilst waiting, the Israelite army is in distress. They are being threatened by the Philistine army, and are in hiding. So, when it hits seven days and Samuel is nowhere to be found, Saul basically takes charge and offers the sacrifices himself. Samuel walks in, just as He is finished. Awkward! Anyhow, we might not think this such a big deal, but the reality is that Saul knows that only the priests could offer the sacrifices. Where did he get off thinking that he could sidestep the rules in order to have favour? Ultimately he was concerned about winning the battle. He disobeyed God's law, because he wanted success. Why did he think that his sacrifice would be acceptable, when it was done with such dishonour? I think he was proud. He didn't really fear God. At the surface he did, because he made the offering. But not deep in his heart. That was just the start. There's a really interesting interplay between fear and pride in this story. On the one hand we might do something out of the fear of man, that actually translates to pride toward God. Interesting, hey? On the other hand, humility with God never translates to pride with people. Except in the case of self-righteousness, which is not true humility at all.

Later, in 1 Samuel 15 God gives a very clear directive that Saul only partially follows. He later retorts that he was afraid of the men and that caused the disobedience. But ultimately it is this last act

YOUR GREATEST TEMPTATION

that causes God to make it very clear that Saul is now rejected as king. But do you think Saul accepted that? Nope! I am not aware of whether a king could abdicate in those days because he probably should have, but he certainly wreaked havoc amongst the Israelites before his death in 1 Samuel 31. Here's just a few:

- He attempts to kill David several times.
  Feeling threatened is no doubt linked to pride. Not to mention that murdering him would have been sinful.
- He hurls a spear at his own son for challenging him.

- He several times charges people with conspiring against him, because they protect David from Saul's attempts to kill an innocent man. Paranoid and an abuse of power.

- He commits a mass murder of priests. 85 priests to be exact. Powerplay, much?

- He bans all mediums from Israel, but then goes and consults one. A leader who thinks he is above his own rules is full of pride.

It is difficult to understand why there is a close relationship between inadequacy, disqualification and pride. But here are a few theories I have...When there is any part of you that actually believes that you have no right to be where you are...you will do anything to protect what you have. Because let's face it, it just seems too good to be true. Disqualification has this counterpart belief: "It's only a matter of time before they all discover that

I am not good enough for this." Everything else becomes collateral damage in the battle toward **security on the throne.** In psychology, it's referred to as the *Imposter Syndrome*[6]. This is the psychological phenomenon where you feel as though you don't deserve your success. Or you feel like you are a fraud and people will eventually find out.

For some of you, ministry success has more to do with validating your leadership than it does growing the kingdom. Maybe this is pressing upon your heart right now, you need to know that God comforts you and is for you. He will not condemn you. But maybe it's time you stopped hiding in the supplies, and acknowledged your fears and repent, so that you can be the best leader for your people and allow leadership to be your worship to God.

Stewardship of power

So how do you steward power?
The goal of stewarding power is to ensure that you have humility in the face of power. So simplistically: Be humble and stay humble. Here are my tips on how to do that:

- **Don't surround yourself with only Christians**
  Christians have a tendency to put people in leadership on a pedestal. Especially Pastors. Some cultures will presume that the prayer of a Pastor is more significant than just the average Christian. At this very moment, my Senior Pastor is a cool, young, intelligent man. He's going to love that I am saying this. He has a few young adult men with massive man-crushes on him. They actually get nervous when he is around. Admittedly, it is really cool that they look up to him so much. Thankfully he is super-humble and none of it has

gone to his head. Whilst there are always people in church who criticise pastors, when you are largely around people who are telling you how awesome you are all the time, or who never disagree with you, you aren't really living in reality. It is possible in this environment to get full of yourself and start to believe that God was lucky to have you. One of the best cures for this is to hang out with people who aren't Christian. Those who don't glorify you. They have no problem cutting you down to size, and they definitely won't praise you for the things that Christians do. My Hindu parents are awesome like this. It never mattered what was going on at church. When I come to my parents' house I'm just the same old Mel. Not Pastor Mel. Hanging out with non-Christians also helps you to have a realistic perspective of life outside of the beehive.

- **Use language that reinforces your position between God and His people**
 This was the most deliberate action I took to deal with pride. I came up with statements that resonated and humbled me, but also reminded me of truths that prevented me from becoming proud. These are a few examples:

    o It's not about you.
    o I didn't earn this. It is God's grace that I get a chance to be a part of it.
    o God it's your church, not mine.
    o I am a disciple first, and a leader second.
    o The first shall be last, and the last shall be first
    o You are a co-labourer, a co-shepherd.

You might find that there are others that are more helpful for you. There are also lots of scriptures about pride that you could memorise. The key is to say them regularly. Because the heart is deceptive, I find you have to verbally say these words to give them the best chance at getting into your heart. It is good for a prideful heart to hear conflicting ideas.

- **Watch your daydreaming**
  What your mind trails off and fantasises about is one of the most indicative aspects of pride. Are you constantly dreaming about yourself on a large stage commanding a massive audience? I don't want to crush your dreams, but that's not always healthy. If you had a vision of it once, relax. But if you are fairly frequently fantasising about yourself in a position of power, influence, or being in anyway worshipped or glorified by your fellow man? Run for the hills! The enemy may be trying to trap you. You should ask yourself why you don't feel like you can exercise power and influence right now. Look, it's not always bad, but just be careful.

- **Be absolutely vulnerable with a few people you can trust**
  If you have no one in your life that you are telling the absolute truth to, you're in danger. And I'm not talking about venting to your spouse. That doesn't count. You need to have people that you are deliberately letting the walls down with, and telling the stuff that you even hide from yourself. Maybe it's being around other people who are really vulnerable with you. When you hear your own failings out loud, it's really hard to think you are God's gift to ministry.

YOUR GREATEST TEMPTATION

- **Listen to yourself**
Literally, listen to what you say. Are they prideful? What would you think if the words you were saying were coming out of someone else's mouth? Would you be labelling them as proud? Would you even want to hang around someone who talks so much about themselves? Out of the abundance of the heart the mouth speaks. Your mouth will tell you a lot about what is going on, if you care to listen to it.

- **Associate with Christians from other churches, visit other churches, and go to conferences**
The biggest problem with working on a church staff, is that you become indoctrinated with your environment. It is absolutely possible to think that there is nothing beyond your church. You become a legend in your own lunchbox. But when you are making an effort to get outside of your own environment, you realise that there are heaps of other people out there who are just as talented or more and just as anointed as you. I love going to conferences when I can, because I am very quickly reminded that my world is very small and there are a lot of people out there trying to build the Kingdom.

- **Who are you feeding? Who does this serve?**
Proud people are self-serving. I have always loved teaching and preaching. But I didn't get to do it a lot when I was a Connect Group Pastor. I can recall meeting with our HR manager at the time, and saying that "I really want to teach!" The HR Manager told me, "Well why don't you use your Connect Group meetings to preach?" My response was "No.

My people don't need to hear another person preach at them. I'm not going to make them attend another midweek meeting just so I can preach". His question was well intentioned, but I knew that doing another meeting would have only served one person...me. What kind of shepherd would I be? I knew how busy my team were, I couldn't do that to them just so I was satisfied.

As leaders, we can convince ourselves that our teams need more programs, more events, or more red tape but really we are just serving ourselves. We create programs that actually revolve more around ourselves than they do around the sheep. Even though ministry is pretty hard, and quite complex, the needs of the sheep are relatively simple. They need to be discipled which is largely done through relationship, prayer and studying the Word. Okay I am grossly oversimplifying. But you get my point. Ask yourself frequently, who is this feeding? Who does this serve? Be honest with yourself, if it's meeting your need more than those you lead... re-evaluate whether it's necessary.

☐ **Ask questions**

I'm not the most intelligent person in the room a lot of the time, so often people say words that I don't understand. Or maybe they are talking about a scripture that I don't fully get. In those scenarios, I resist all urges to laugh along, and apply the courage to say, "what does that word mean?" Or "I don't understand, could you explain it?". If I don't know the answer to a question I say, "I don't know". I do this more for my sake rather than theirs because honestly people can act pretty condescendingly when you don't know something they do.

Doing this I hope never to be so proud that I don't have the humility to learn and grow in front of those from whom I seek approval. I am also releasing the pressure internally that says I should know. Who said I should know everything?? God didn't!! That's a pressure as leaders we put on ourselves. I'm not saying that we shouldn't grow and learn, but the desire to know everything sounds very similar to a conversation in the Garden of Eden. Humble people will ask questions, whilst proud people care about image and how they are perceived too much to even consider asking a question, lest they admit they don't know something.

- **Treat those you would want the approval of, the way you would treat the cleaner**

I personally think that the person who does the least status-oriented job in your church, the cleaner, is the most awesome person in your church. Think about it, they do their task in virtual invisibility. They pick up your trash, keeping your secrets, and largely they don't get a thank you. That is a servant heart.

Unfortunately, everywhere I've worked the cleaner is the least appreciated and often not even acknowledged. My Dad who is an incredible leader and not at all a Christian, but often demonstrates the most incredible 'Christian' values, demonstrated to me very early in life to treat those who are serving you with respect and honour. He would always talk to the waitresses and treat them respectfully. Although I think my mum was suspicious that he was chatting them up. He would acknowledge them when they came to the table, he would say thank you, smile, and tip them if they served like they loved their job. What an example he set for me?! He showed me that what you really think about people, will be demonstrated by how you treat the 'least'.

Pride can often vouch for position and power. Which naturally means it will treat those that you perceive as valuable to your cause for position and power, with greater blessing, charm etc. etc. Something that I have tried to do, is to treat those 'influencers' the same as I would the cleaner. Which either means you start to treat the cleaner better, or you treat the 'influencer' like a real person.

Final thoughts...

The last thing any of us want to do is become modern day Pharisees. But if we aren't careful, it's actually all too easy. Everything written here about pride could be said of the Pharisees. They were so full of themselves. Their faith was a show (Matthew 6:1), their righteousness was motivated by self-love, power and control. For people so knowledgeable in the Word of God, they completely missed the Messiah even when He was right before them. How many times have you missed what God was doing because you were building your own empire? How many times will you miss an opportunity to partner with what He is doing, because your pride has taken your eyes off the goal? I want to see revival, but I think we keep looking for what it has looked like in the past. But if God is bringing revival, it's going to look different. Are you going to see this new move of the Spirit? Because the humble will see it. The proud won't.

The Jesus factor

In direct contrast to the Pharisees is Jesus. The real deal. I know of no greater steward of power than Jesus. The one who truly holds the power of heaven in His hands. He who comes to earth and serves. He remained humble in spite of knowing He was the Messiah. He could have asked for the biggest, fattest, richest seat in society, with all the indulgences and luxuries, by simply announcing himself to the Jews. The greatest aspect that illuminates my mind to Jesus' stewardship of power, is the fact that He came to earth and did nothing to partner with the worlds powerful. He didn't align with the Pharisees. He didn't come alongside the Romans. He didn't care to have His photo with the famous of this earth. Instead He spent his days with prostitutes, lepers, and the rejects of society. The people nobody wanted to associate with. The kind of people who would cause your congregation to say "Oh, why are they hanging out with Him?" He used His supernatural power to serve. He entered the places that we often won't dare to. He didn't have a special car space. He didn't have reserved seating. Being the Messiah didn't cause Him to see himself as entitled to any kind of special treatment. In fact, He died a gruesome, embarrassing and humiliating death, like a common criminal. There wasn't an inch of pride in Him. He was all purity and humility. It's not that He wasn't to be tempted by it though. The enemy comes to Him in the desert, where He is fasting, and does two things to tempt Him:

- He tempts Him to prove himself.
- He tempts Him with power and worship.

Jesus declines both. He knows He doesn't have to prove himself. Why would you when you know who you are? Pride is all too consumed with showing off. But that's not what Jesus is about. He wasn't on earth to show off His power. Any power He had was used to do good for others: heal, feed, teach, share, serve, give, encourage and love.

When you know the power you have, like Jesus, you know that you don't need to use it. This is the heart of the humble. You are more interested in giving it away for the benefit of others. Power that is hoarded and power that is used to lord over and control, is the type of power the enemy specialises in, and was ultimately the only kind of power he could offer Jesus. And Jesus never demanded authority or submission, not like King Saul. He just walked and lived knowing He had it. May we be like this! May we realise that power is not given to advantage us. It's been given to enable us to serve. May we be more interested in the rejects of society, rather than the ones who make us feel significant and important. Those who we might want to put on our Instagram story. May we become great stewards of power, and resist pride at every turn.

CHAPTER 3

Pastors be talkin'

There's a famous movie that I watched as a youngster, called *The Nutty Professor*[7]. There's this scene that has a young black comedian, whose entire routine is to point out an audience member and absolutely tease them for their imperfections. Besides that, he has one line that he repeats in lieu of finding some poor victim: "Women be shopping! You can't stop a woman from shopping!" It's so ridiculous...and obviously, you are meant to dislike him, because later Eddie Murphy roasts him. But when I was thinking about writing this chapter, that line came to mind: "Pastors be talkin'! You can't stop a pastor from talking!"

Gone are the days when a pastor would teach for hours on end. And I for one am pretty happy about that. But I know that there would be many an older pastor who wished those glory days were back. Instead they have to reduce a message to 40 minutes or 25 minutes, and lose content they would have loved to talk about.

So, here's the point: Pastors love to talk. So much so, that the ones who don't talk so much often wonder whether they are supposed

> We might deal with highly **spiritual** matters, but we are also **practical** beings.

to be pastors. Can I get an 'Amen' from my introverted Pastors out there? The modern pastor would perceive their role as largely centred around communication, and whilst it certainly is a big part of the role, I think the scales have tipped a bit too much in one direction.

For a lot of you, this topic is not really a big deal. In many ways, I am writing this for people who are experiencing the extreme of this. Because when it is extreme it is annoying, and it makes the organisation ineffective. So, apologies if this chapter doesn't help everyone in your specific context. Hopefully, it simply affirms you in your current situation.

2 Steps forward, 2 steps back

I got to give it to pastors. Most of the time they have had absolutely no business training including setting vision, mission or goal. And yet some pastors, due to the size of their churches probably require more of these skills than being able to teach. Thankfully a lot of the theological training institutions are now including these units of study. A few years into my role leading the Connect Groups, I had been writing up a strategy that would give some guidance to leaders on discipleship. I was vaguely aware that the Executive team was writing a model for discipleship, and so I thought I would check in on its status so that I could include it in my document. Anyhow, I went and chatted with one of the pastors involved with the discussion. I was excited! This was an area that was going to be really helpful for my leaders. Especially with new Christians getting into groups, and some of our leaders inviting non-believers to their groups. However, I was so disappointed to find out that the discussion hadn't been finalised.

In fact, the discussion had been going on for about six months, with no evidence of anything being put to paper and the hold-up centred on a few specific words. Additionally, when I asked for the anticipated timeframe for completion, there was none, and they didn't want to put a timeframe on it. In other words, I couldn't proceed with my document and I had no idea how long I was going to have to put that on hold. What a disempowering position to be in. In my zeal to see some progress on the matter, I offered to write something up myself for the Connect Group Leaders, that they could hack at. My experience being, that sometimes when the ball isn't quite rolling, it's better to have something to critique than to have a clean slate. But they weren't keen on this either. They did eventually come out with a discipleship model, but of course it was after a really long time and it didn't revolutionise discipleship in our church. Why in the world did it take so long? From my observations, the few pastors involved actually believed that having the perfect wording would be the difference between whether people engaged in discipleship. That's how significant the wording is. I don't blame them in a way, because all the communication philosophies tell you that for something to be retained it has to be memorable. But sometimes the reason they aren't being embraced, is not because of the words. It's because of what is or isn't being done.

Feed and care

Like many leaders, I have spent so much time in John 21:15-17. Jesus deliberately says that we must feed and care for the sheep and lambs if we love Him. Most articles and papers I've read suggest that the Word of God is the material we are to feed them. And thus, we focus on teaching the Word of God as central to the Church, and I certainly don't disagree with the centrality of the Word. But every commentary I've read on this passage, also suggests that equal attention is paid to the care of the sheep. Additionally, wherever the shepherds of Israel were being chastised by God for their treatment of the sheep, with the exception of maybe one passage…it was their care that was under question, not necessarily the teaching. In Ezekiel and Jeremiah, the passages focus on the sheep being lost, abandoned and scattered. There injuries weren't being cared for. Such behaviours motivated God to withdraw the shepherds, and for God to take over the role of being the Shepherd for His people. Then you have Jesus who enters, and calls himself the Good Shepherd. This was meant to indicate Gods completion of this prophecy.

Whilst many a pastor may spend 10-15 hours preparing a message for a Sunday. Not to mention the copious hours spent on the Sunday experience: meetings for the order of service, meetings about worship, meetings about New People spaces. We are hard stretched to see the same amount of time being spent on caring. Admittedly, in a big church your congregation will diminish if the Senior Pastor spends all of his time meeting with the congregation members. Just ask Carey Nieuwhof, founding pastor of Connexus Church in Barrie, Ontario. My point is that for the most part, very little time is spent working out systems that will ensure the care of the sheep, and the departments that would help care for the sheep are often secondary to the departments that have a 'Sunday' focus (i.e. Pastoral Care or Small Groups). Now let me get something straight, I am not addressing this because I have a bee in my bonnet about my own personal experience as the Small Group Pastor. My conviction comes from a place of wanting to be a good shepherd who both feeds and cares for the sheep. I did the best I could to feed and care for my sheep. But often I felt like I was warring against the Sunday beast, that would be saturated with resources and time, whilst the departments focused on general caring were struggling to be equipped for their task. As though the three-minute eye darting conversations pastors have with a congregation member on a Sunday, would actually suffice for a broken person on the edge.

In God's eyes, our actions are just as important as our words. More specifically, in God's eyes, our caring is just as important as our teaching. In God's eyes, the activation of the Word is just as important as the Word itself. This all vaguely reminds me of James 1:22 where we are encouraged not to be listeners only, but to be doers of the Word. I am sure that this message has been preached to your congregation members because we are often convinced that they aren't doing enough...if only we would look at the log in our own eye first!

We often tell them to evangelise more, and yet our relationships are exclusively made up of our church community. Possibly leading to severed friendships with our old non-believing friends. We are telling them to love people more, and yet we go home to families that often don't feel loved. I'm included in this.

It might help understand where I am coming from, if I describe a few more places where this focus on words has become a bit unbalanced.

Other manifestations...

- **Preaching is the epitome**
  Sadly, there is a whole generation of young leaders, who are all bucking for a chance to preach. If you are new to ministry, I could pretty safely guess that you too would like to preach. I was the same. I say sadly though, because I don't see the same number of leaders wanting to shepherd, care or serve. Annoyingly, we pastors try to correct this attitude because experience tells us that there are some people who want to be on the platform for the wrong reasons. But we would be wise to check our own hearts, and consider the example we have been setting for these young leaders. Preaching is a highly visible role and no doubt there will always be some glory given to it for that reason. But the kingdom culture is one that encourages anonymity (Matthew 6) and serving without visibility. Jesus frequently refers to the greatest being the one who serves. His intention was that Christian leadership be marked by service. In John 13, He sets an example for His disciples to follow when He washes their feet - a job usually reserved for the slave of the house. I know many preachers who serve their people. But I know many more looking for opportunities to preach, over opportunities to serve. And I certainly ask the question, who is encouraging that behaviour?

- **Over-emphasis on the 'why' in preaching**
  WHAT??? Okay, some of you are freaking out right now. I do agree, that it is important to give people sound reasoning. Although generations before were not always like this. People

generally want to understand why God says what He does. And if our 'why' is convincing enough, it may cause people to be open to change. What I find problematic, is that we often spend so much time establishing the 'why' that there is very little practical advice as to how to do anything about it. The practical advice is a quick two-liner, often vague, at the end of a message. Or it's a response moment, when the preacher can pray. However, if a message really moves someone, they want to know what they can do about it. People are tired of hearing the cliched Christian answers, too - pray about it, pray more, read your Bible…oh, and Jesus. We might deal with highly spiritual matters, but we are also practical beings. If you think that the objective of a good message is to sell a good 'why', I would argue that you haven't had your listeners in mind. Did you know a good chunk of the population don't want a good 'why'? I've worked with labourers and I've worked with engineers. I know that with the engineers, I had to anticipate every question, which includes the 'How'. 'How does the system work?' 'How will I get paid?' 'How do they work out what I will get paid?' But with the labourers, they often didn't care that much about the why or the 'How' - they just wanted the 'What'. 'What do I need to sign?' 'What time do I need to be there?' 'What's that?' How much are we alienating people when we preach if we think it's all about understanding a concept, and not learning how to activate it.

So how does this relate to a focus on words? A message that can't be activated, is arguably not teaching at all. It assumes that we just want to collect ideas, but not do anything with them. What was it for, if the people don't understand how to apply it? Well, I think the 'why' focus can reveal that our desire for preaching, can sometimes be about us and how we are perceived. We can be more consumed by impressing people with an inspiring message...the fact is, practical points about application are often mundane. They don't have the Holy Spirit flavour that we like to communicate. We'd rather be crouched on the floor like Steven Furtick at Hillsong Conference 2016, when he was re-enacting Paul and Silas worshipping in the prison. EPIC! INSPIRING! We think that's what everyone wants from us too, because they listen to Furtick's podcasts. If we are honest, sometimes preaching is more for us than it is for them.

- **Lots of meetings**
I can't stand this! When I worked in corporate, I would have maybe one or two mandatory weekly meetings. We had more money at stake, and just as many people at stake for our decisions. I worked with people who had injuries, often psychological with a long-term history of unemployment. Their future was often highly influenced by how well we managed their case. But we were able to be succinct with our meetings. Our productivity and results were amazing. One of my workplaces, had a weekly half hour meeting hearing from about ten team members. It never went over time, it was focused, it never felt rushed and it was effective. In church though, it seems like every day is just chock full of meetings. Whether it's a problem or an issue, an idea or a concept... everything warrants a meeting. The more 'important' you are, the more meetings you'll be in too. Sometimes you would

meet three or five times over exactly the same matter, and say exactly the same things. What a nightmare for productivity. Surely it is not necessary to have this many meetings. I'm not talking about Pastoral Care meetings either. Most pastors who work in settings like the one I worked in, find it so hard to fit Pastoral Care meetings in. Often they are taking copious amounts of work home because the day is full of meetings. I believe this does stem in part from the importance that is put on talking through issues. We overvalue talking and think that we simply must talk about everything. And yet the irony is that the communication is often so poor in churches. So many of these issues don't get disseminated. The really critical and important factors don't get talked about. I've realised that a lot of the time it's because pastors lack the self-control over their mouths and simply must be heard on every matter. Yeah that's right, it applies to your tongue too...go read Proverbs for a massive wake up call on wise handling of the tongue. The truth is that communication is not always for the benefit of the communicator.

☐ **Meetings running overtime**
I'm not really sure why meetings need to regularly go overtime, but they do. True, this can be very dependent on who is running the meeting. I've noticed that a lot of the allocated time is spent on people expressing their viewpoint, rather than identifying the specific actions. So, in the last two minutes of the meeting, you are essentially trying to figure out how to fix the issue. It would be extremely helpful if meetings had an agenda, which just makes good planning sense. I presume

with so many meetings, writing agendas for each one would be very time consuming. Also, people don't necessarily stick to the agenda, including the chair. But having less meetings with agendas, is still more effective than having lots of meetings with no agenda.

- **Pastoral care**

    Pastoral care is actually really important. Particularly to God. However, there are times when the pastor can think that all they need to do is say the right thing to fix a person's problem. Unfortunately, pastoral care isn't really that simple and the objective is not necessarily to fix the matter OR even to talk. The focus of pastoral care is the caring. Which sometimes is talking, but again, not necessarily. That may mean that the best thing you can do is to be there for someone. It may mean that the best thing you can do is to pray. Care is a vague term, and in some ways I think deliberately so. Because it was never meant to turn into a box you can tick on your 'successful pastoring' list. There are times too that pastoral care cannot do the work of a good group of Christian friends or a Counsellor or Psychologist.

- **Overemphasis on Sundays**

    For the average congregation member, a Sunday service is about 1.5 hours out of a 168-hour week (not even 1% of the week). We are putting a lot of pressure on a Sunday, if we think that it's going to transform a person the way the early church did. The truth is, it's pretty exceptional that amazing things do happen in 1.5 hours. But if we aren't careful we can worship the method of Sunday services over the God who is faithful to His people and will show up at every opportunity we give Him...literally every opportunity. This includes

> When done out of service to God, **mankind** will be **grateful** for God's and our **presence** in society

a simple coffee with friends. As leaders in a church, it can feel like Sunday is the game day. And in fact, I think I have heard that terminology used by Pastors. I don't love it. It's not helpful, because it diminishes the work that is done during the week: catch-ups, phone calls, small groups. It also diminishes the value of the lives our congregation members are living for God during the week. Some of the 'during the week' work the real reason people are coming back to your church. For believers, EVERYDAY IS GAME DAY. And they are all of equal value in God's' sight. So how does a focus on words, create an overemphasis on Sundays? If I were to sit down and watch a team of leaders put together an order of service, I can identify very quickly the focal point of a Sunday service. It's the preaching. Whilst we value worship, most leaders will talk about worship in terms of preparing people's hearts for the message. Announcements are put before the message, because we want the message to be remembered. We often encourage prayer at the end for the activation of the message. When we podcast, it's the message that is shared. Now I don't disagree with this as the message is important. But Sunday services are not synonymous with the Word. The Word is shared when people do a Bible Study together. When friends encourage each other over the Word. I would argue that the Word being reflected on and reinforced throughout the week is just as meaningful as the Word being preached. Especially with a culture that has steered away from notetaking in services. Often people are leaving a service, never to again consider the message they heard. Anyhow, I slightly digress. My point is to say that the Word is powerful, and we should be encouraged to engage our church members to have it central throughout their week rather than emphasise the Sunday as the exclusive place of learning. Who knows? Maybe this over-emphasis on Sundays, is actually part of the reason congregation members don't attend as frequently as they once did? It doesn't take too long for a congregation member to realise that Sundays don't meet every need. They aren't supposed to, of course. But if we sell it like it does…maybe they just don't buy our marketing anymore. I know this is a way more complex issue than that, but it's just a thought.

- **Over-communication in services**
When Sundays becomes the main method of ministry to church members, inevitably we try to fit as much as communication as we can into it. I actually prefer preaching to leading a meeting. Because there is so much to be achieved leading a meeting is quite a complex task these days. Sometimes you are trying to encourage a greater engagement in the worship, if the worship leader hasn't already brought a word. Then you are trying to transition out of worship without losing the atmosphere, which may involve a 30 second message involving scripture and an inspiring prayer. Then it's engaging the congregation in

talking to each other, often for the sake of new people. Then it's welcoming, announcements that you have to 'sell'. You may have a short tithing message and occasionally you will interview people. If the leader of the meeting wraps up the service, you are also reminding people of last-minute sign ups, prayer and anything else that is deemed critical. There is so much verbal communication. Unfortunately, the reality of communication is that when there's too much communication it blurs the important stuff. As preachers we understand the need for focus and clarity in our messages, because we acknowledge that over-communication could detract from our main points. However, we don't necessarily translate that same principle to the overall service. Why? Because so much is riding on the Sunday service to achieve everything. Now I could tell you my thoughts on how to resolve this, but that's not really the purpose of this book. It is suggested that you read Simple Church[8] if you want some expert advice. It's simply to raise the point that we've become very reliant on words to achieve everything.

☐ **Evangelism = Bring your friends to church!**
Bringing people to church is a great idea. But I know, for my Hindu parents who consider every religious institution sacred, I will probably never see them walk through those doors as Hindus. Why have we dwindled evangelism down to attending a church service? Doesn't the Great Commission say "GO"? Is this partly because we think that if we could just get a person into the doors and they see how amazing our service is, and they are emotionally moved by the worship, and they hear

God's Word…that they may receive Christ? Maybe. But why are we teaching our people to make them come only, instead of teaching them to go? Evangelism is not really something I've spent a lot of time researching, so maybe I've missed something. I think the part that is a bit doctrinally conflicting is that at the same time we are trying to teach people that they are now the temple of the Holy Spirit. He lives in you! Oh, but don't rely on the Holy Spirit when you are out in the world, to pray with people and see them receive Christ! Bring them to church, because the spirit of God is more powerful there! WHAT?? It's the same spirit! The power is not in the location, or in the message, or in the worship. It's in the Spirit. This 'bring your friends to church' message can affect believers' confidence to share Jesus, because they start to believe that the gospel isn't enough. That they need the church experience to be saved. We unintentionally project our evangelism formula onto the congregation, and unfortunately it doesn't always lead to a greater trust in the Holy Spirit.

- **Prayer becomes another opportunity to preach**

  As leaders, we often feel like it's our responsibility to create an atmosphere of faith through our prayer. A faith filled prayer meeting is so awesome. But in our zeal to 'manufacture' atmosphere we can often turn prayer into something other than what it was designed for. Prayer, in any form, is still primarily communication between us and God. Instead, it can feel like another sermon intended to engage the people instead of engaging Him. The worst part of this is the fact that we can unknowingly prevent others from praying in front of each other. We unintentionally put this expectation on those around us that prayer is like a sermon. People don't need any more motivation to be afraid of each other's judgement. But insisting that our prayer is profound and articulate, is certainly not helping. Why do we do that? Because we still think that what we say can change the atmosphere from one of apathy to faith. And sometimes it can. But not always. If we want faith filled prayer meetings, we ought to rely on real faith and discipleship that happens during the week. Make prayer really simple and accessible, that all may feel confident to do it. Of all the people I know who are afraid to pray in public, its largely because they are nervous about people judging what they say. How did we communicate that the fundamental component of prayer, is how it is said? If you don't think so, listen to someone praying for healing. We couldn't make it clearer that we think there is a 'special' way to pray to release healing. It wouldn't be GOD'S healing power, if it relied on a formula. Jesus and His disciples often only said two words to heal a person: *'Be healed!'* (Matt 8:3, NLT) Prayer is powerful, and it doesn't rely on the right words to make it work. At times, say very little, and allow it to sound unfinished. Only say that which is necessary, and set the example to those around you that they don't have to be profound when they speak.

These are just a few ways in which communication or words can give an imbalanced value.

But here's the flip side. Words are actually powerful! Our God himself spoke the world and His creation into being. So many of the people we live alongside are a product of the words that either they or others have spoken over them. Words are powerful.

But so is silence.

The truth is lots of actions are powerful when done in the right timing. Hospitality is powerful…if it's with the right timing. An act of service is powerful…in the right timing. Discernment is powerful…in the right timing. As Ecclesiastes 3 says, *'there is a time for everything.'* Which means it's not always time for talking. Which means that relying on the power of a 'word' to change something, is not always wise. On the other hand, this should release a little pressure for leaders too. You don't have to be petrified about saying the wrong thing. You don't have to fix a situation by saying the perfect words. You don't really even have to fix everything which was never a part of the deal anyway. There may be a reason we focus on words, and it's not necessarily related to the power of the Word…

Emotions speak louder than words

As a youth leader, a connection was made with a young adult girl. Not long after I got to know her, my husband and I made the big move interstate. One of my leaders continued to journey with her, but after about a year the girl was no longer attending church amongst other changes in behaviour. I was coming back for a visit, and the leader let me know that the girl, after some convincing was agreeable to catching up. The leader asked me if I wanted to come along whilst I was visiting. So, as I sat and listened to her answer our questions, I noticed a recurring theme. She was constantly using words and phrases that indicated that her emotions were guiding her every decision. It was very obvious. Eventually, I got a little frustrated and decided to gently confront this very unstable guide she was relying on. I said to her something like, "A relationship is not always about feeling, it's also about conviction. If you believe in God, and you believe Him at His Word, you'll follow and obey regardless of how you are feeling because you know it's the truth." She seemed pretty shocked. Maybe it was a bit harsh, but I had been validating every feeling she had all night and it wasn't proving helpful. This certainly got her attention. She didn't come back to church, but at least she made a choice, which God would rather than her being lukewarm. I stand by my words. If marriages were all about how we feel, none of them would ever last. At some point, the commitment you've made is what keeps you faithful. It's the same with God. The problem is, that we don't always communicate this with our people. One concerning aspect of the Western church is the reliance on emotion to motivate. If emotion is the only way we can obey God, we are in trouble. The persecuted church would probably think this is quite immature. Unfortunately, the use of emotion can create a cyclical effect. People are motivated by their feelings, and then leaders are forced to appeal to feelings to keep people engaged. Thus, enter the significance of words and communication.

The quickest way to change how people feel, is to say something that they probably want to hear, or something that makes them feel good. As a counsellor, I know all too well the words you can say to change an atmosphere or a person's feelings. I'm not kidding, it's actually really easy. It is really easy to manipulate people, which is why I am so careful about what

I say. But any change motivated by feelings is not going to last. Just like the husband who promises to change and let go of that relationship, or addiction, because he doesn't want his wife to leave. It's so rare that he will actually follow through, if his reaction is rooted in emotion. It will probably last until the next time the individual faces something hard, and comes back to you to hear you say something else that will inspire them again. Leaders don't want that kind of dependency, that prohibits people from learning to stand on their own two feet. We ought to want them to read the Bible for themselves. To pray for themselves, not wait for powerful prayers at the end of each week by a church leader. They'll be like vulnerable sheep, an easy prey, during the week if they don't learn that faith is not an emotion. In this framework, people run from the hard stuff missing an opportunity to grow. Sometimes our desire to be life-giving, and give hope, are actually more about making people feel a certain way rather than giving them truth that sets them free. Just think about Matthew 7:13-14…

> *"Enter by the narrow gate; for wide is the gate and broad is the way that leads to destruction, and there are many who go in by it. Because narrow is the gate and difficult is the way which leads to life, and there are few who find it." (NKJV)*

Forget about the salvation theology in this passage for a second. 'Narrow' simply implies hardship and trouble. It referred to the pressing of grapes. From this we can deduce at the very least, that the Christian path, the narrow path, is full of hardship. Jesus is promising it to be a harder life. In fact, it wasn't supposed to make life easier. It's a costly life. As leaders, if we are going to motivate people to access the narrow gate we will need more than our words and good feelings. Words won't necessarily lead a person to take up their cross.

If we really think about it. This feeling-based decision making, is quite worldly. That's what happens in the world. Feelings dictate who you hang around, who you marry, your profession, what clothes you wear...there are still remnants of other influences, of course. Values. Morals. These factors do still have a place in society. But feelings and emotions are very significant influencers. It is the crux of why society is seeking happiness. The desire for a happy, financially secure life, is all about feelings. Now, feelings and emotions aren't the enemy!! Please don't let that be your take away. Feelings and emotions are a creation of God himself, which He also has. We just haven't necessarily learnt how to appropriately process emotions, for the betterment of ourselves, and society. It wouldn't be right to present a five-step plan for processing emotions here. This is definitely not my area of expertise. But find resources or speak to a counsellor to grow in this area.

Possibly the most concerning part of this is the fact that this belief and attitude has seeped into many leaders. We have been sowing these 'what's in it for me?' messages, and emotionally motivating seeds because it's often the lens we are looking through. We talk about a feeling of peace, which sometimes is just a desire for comfort. I'll put my hand up and say that I am guilty too. We care about how people are going to feel, because we are focused on feelings.

The biggest sign of this is our belief about having an experience with God. It's not wrong that we want to feel God. Even if it is just to have that reassurance sometimes that He actually exists. I am all too empathetic to the multitude of Christians who just find it so hard to relate and love a being who we can't see or feel. And as leaders we should definitely be trying to grow and learn how we can help people in this place, because it's not up to us or them whether God decides to reveal Himself through a supernatural experience. The Pentecostals might find this really hard to believe, but some people never have an experience of God. It's not because they are not faithful, or don't understand the Holy Spirit. And we certainly should ask ourselves why a lot of leaders believe that a person can't love God fully without an experience. Particularly agape love which has very little to do with emotion.

But, I'm going to say it...encountering God is not the goal of our ministry. So many leaders say that all people need is an encounter with God. Where did that theology come from? Here's the evidence that this is simply not true. Solomon encountered God twice. There was the first occasion when God asked Him what He wanted (1 Kings 3). And then there was the second occasion where God instructed Him to be faithful (1 Kings 9). He literally saw God twice. But even that couldn't have stopped him from falling away on account of his wayward wives. We read passages about Paul, who has a miraculous encounter with God and presume that this means experiences change people. Yeah, well sometimes. In most cases, it's just the starting point. The detail we miss about Paul though, is that He was a very different man to Solomon. He was already a man of conviction and obedience before he met Jesus. Then He met the real Messiah, the one He would also have been waiting for. It changed what He was obeying. Paul surrendered everything because of Jesus.

Not because of the experience. An encounter still can't do what discipleship does. Experiences aren't that powerful. Feelings are fickle. Words can't achieve everything. Real change comes from daily carrying your cross, and surrendering just that bit more than you did the day before.

Deeds

The problem is that whilst we are focused on inspiring words and good feelings, God is focused on other aspects. Our deeds are really important to God. And that goes beyond preaching the gospel. This isn't supposed to create legalistic behaviours, because the Old Testament also reminds us that God did not love all the offerings the people of Israel were bringing. The heart behind an offering matters. They are supposed to come from an honest and genuine love and faith in God, that compels us to live a life of worship and sacrifice for His Kingdom. Our love and faith in God is supposed to translate to action, otherwise was it really love and faith at all? Hey, don't shoot the messenger! It was James who said, *"show me your faith without deeds and I will show you my faith BY my deeds"* in James 2:18. In Revelations, there are 7 letters to the churches and 6 of them begin in a very similar way:

> *"I know your deeds"*

This is the general theme of each address. Jesus doesn't remark about their beautiful worship, their understanding of the Word or the number of verses they memorised. He wasn't remarking on how long they spent praying or reading the Word, or how many sermon podcast's they listened to. It doesn't mean that God doesn't like these aspects of Christian living, but this is not what was getting His attention. It was their actions. Whether in service to each other, or the world. Deeds, also translated as works or labour in other places, refers to how we treat our employer, how we serve our fellow believers, how we serve the poor and disadvantaged, generosity, having good character and integrity, how we love and serve the unlovable, sharing your possessions…to basically serve God and people wholeheartedly wherever you are. Those are deeds! Unfortunately, we are often a few steps behind measuring our heart and love by our intentions…

According to scripture, these good deeds are actually capable of causing non-believers to praise God. When done out of service to God, mankind will be grateful for God's and our presence in society. This would be a wonderfully refreshing and stark contrast to what our society presently thinks of us. What an epic vision of the co-labouring between church and God! We were ALWAYS meant to be known for our deeds and the good we would bring to our world.

So, my encouragement is to get the balance back. Our job isn't to preach or make people feel good through our use of carefully constructed words and statements. It's to model a life of worship and good deeds for our community so they would follow our example and make a difference in this world.

Fruit

So, what do we do to change all of this? Or to stay focused? We need to change what we measure. Many of us for way too long, have assessed Pastors and leaders by their passionate charismatic preaching and the number of people who attend their church. At the time of writing Galatians, Paul was particularly concerned about the false prophets and false apostles. It was Paul, inspired by the spirit of God who encouraged that church community to identify the fruit of the Spirit, in order to ascertain a person's heart. For most of my childhood, I fully believed that this fruit was something we were to strive toward to prove ourselves to God. To my surprise, as a young adult I discovered that this was supposed to be our test as to whether we should believe a prophet or an apostle. We were to look at their lives. The proof of the Spirit's presence. Were they loving, joyful, peaceful, patient, kind, gentle, good, faithful and self-controlled? Remember, anyone can say anything. What if we were to make this our measure? Not in words, but in deed. What if rather than rating ourselves as preachers, and our specific wording or impact, we were to ask:

- Was I loving to my people today? Did I sacrificially serve them and God? Did I get up and do those acts of service I didn't want to do, because I love them? And not because I want them to think better of me?

- Was I joyful in my dealings? Did I take that bad news from my leader with joy? Did I show them how to have joy despite the circumstances?

- Was I peaceful? Did I work in a way that promoted peace in my interactions? Did I make an effort to reconcile with others today?

- Was I patient with the new Christian who keeps falling off the horse? With the leader who keeps making mistakes? Was I patient with my family?

- Was I kind to the person in need on the sidewalk? To the person who can do nothing for me? Did I show kindness to the person who disappointed me?

- Was I faithful? To my people, to God, to my family or spouse? To the vision?

- Was I gentle when I listened? When I corrected? When I was annoyed?

- Was I good to those I led today? Did I demonstrate God's' goodness in their lives?

- Was I self-controlled? Did I hold my tongue when I should have? Was I slow to react when I was angry today?

I'm not talking about whether you said loving, patient and kind words. Or whether you FELT loving, patient and kind. I know people who think they are the most loving relational people, and they couldn't be more wrong. It doesn't matter what you feel or say. It matters what you did. Was it, evidence of the Spirit's presence in your life? To your employees, and your leaders, and…YOUR FAMILY? Don't get freaked out. We are all a work in progress. I'm feeling a little stressed looking at that list too. I am simply saying, let's change the success measure as leaders. Let's stop worshipping those guys and girls on great big stages with massive audiences preaching like there is a fire about to be ignited by their words, and start praising those who are serving in hard places in anonymity who are still leading with great character and great fruit. Let's bring the balance back.

The Jesus factor
What was it like for Jesus? How did he manage it?
When you look through the gospels, Jesus taught a lot. Often what He said would probably not have always been profound to His listeners. It was either simple, like that of the parables or utterly confusing. But some of the most revolutionary characteristics about Jesus were His actions. He ate with the rejects of society, He cried, He prayed, He fed, He washed the feet of His disciples. Most significantly of all, He died on the cross, enduring an awful and humiliating death for us. Nothing that Jesus said would have really meant that much, if it weren't for His final act on the cross. The cross validated everything He taught. In Gethsemane, when He asks if there is another way, in spite of His feelings, He obeys. He follows through in action and commitment, the love that He professed to have for His Father and us. If you ask yourself, how you have seen the faithfulness of God in your life, you would no doubt refer to the different merciful acts that He has done for you. He provided you with a job and a future. He gave you that spouse you've been praying for. He gave you that child that you weren't sure you could have. He provided the money for that surgery. He healed that sickness. The details may be different, but the stories are largely the same. A merciful God acts for us. The Servant

> The **cross** validated everything He taught

King is still serving us. Our measure of God's faithfulness is His actions. God's faithfulness is seen through His deeds, and fulfilling His words. Not through words alone. May we all seek to live a faithful life, of service and good deeds that the generations may follow our example and bring God's presence into our communities.

CHAPTER 4

Meeting your capacity

In the first year of working at the church, I felt invincible. I was working crazy hours, but I wasn't overly concerned. I had done long hours before in previous jobs, I didn't think I would need to change that. I just was so excited about finally being in ministry after ten years of God redirecting me. I couldn't get enough. I had a Connect Group and was doing Creative meetings in addition to the all-church events. I would be in the office really early, and would regularly leave later than I had planned. I was often at two services on a Sunday, even though I didn't need to be. Another leader encouraged me early in the piece to promise my family Sunday night at home. I always felt like I was missing out when I wasn't at night services. And when I was there it almost felt like adrenaline. I knew it would only be a matter of time, until I was attending the night services too.

Everything was going so well, and with great momentum. Until I got to the Women's Conference later that year. There had been some doubts over certain items, and the Senior Pastor's wife was

> Being 'busy' doesn't at all mean you are leading well, or heading in the **right** direction

very particular about the conference. So, I basically turned up at almost every rehearsal. That equated to almost two weeks straight of nights out, along with full weekends. No one asked me to, I just decided that I would. The week before a conference is usually a write off anyway. But I attended extra little rehearsals that were happening throughout the week. I was just so eager to have everything go according to the well devised plan. Plus, I didn't need a lot of extra motivation. I loved what I was doing. I couldn't believe that I was paid to do what I was doing. The conference was a success, as always. In the afternoon of the conference, when it was all over, I came home and completely crashed for hours on the couch. My husband let me rest and took my daughter out. I was up early the next day, ready to serve with the team at our Sunday services. Everything was fine until I was exiting through the front door. Just as I was closing the door, I could hear my two year old daughter running and screaming. "MUMMY DON'T LEAVE ME!!!!" It was a gut-wrenching cry. She didn't understand that I was serving God! All she knew was that she missed me terribly, and she wanted to be with me. I had hardly spent any time with her. And the time I did have, I was slouched on the couch, allowing her to safely entertain herself. I closed the door, standing outside, able to hear her desperate cry. I knew this cry was different. 'What are you doing?' I asked myself…with tears welling up in my eyes.

For the next few months, instead of being in my boss's office talking about ideas and exciting developments, I spent hours in tears telling her that I wasn't sure how much longer I could maintain this pace. I lost faith badly. In myself. In my circumstances.

Definitely in my ability to juggle it all. Inevitably something was going to be sacrificed in my attempts to have it all. I started to ask questions as to whether I was even supposed to be in ministry. This went on for months. The Christmas Production, I knew I would be producing, was fast approaching. I was arriving most days, lamenting about quitting. I felt like I needed to make a decision to quit with plenty of time before the Christmas Show. I didn't want to leave people scrambling to put the show together as a result of my dropping the ball. In the planning meeting for Christmas, I had come painfully close to a panic attack, but battled through it. Frequently keeping my head above water with self-talk; it wouldn't have taken much for me to be overwhelmed and enveloped by a panic attack. I gave God a timeframe, which is something I have done a fair few times in my life. Our church movement State conference was coming up, and so I told God "Unless something really significant happens at this conference. Unless I hear really clearly from you, I will quit my job when I return from the conference." Well, it turns out that God heard. The conference was a massive turn around. I did hear from God. In so many unusual ways. He is so faithful. I returned to work, knowing that I could make it. And I did. And the show was a complete success! But after the show was over, I had to strategise my new life. If I was going to continue in ministry, I had to figure out some better ways of managing this new lifestyle.

"Let me introduce you to your capacity!!"

When most people talk about capacity, they are generally referring to a person's ability to complete tasks whether in their personal life or in their jobs. A person's capacity generally changes and adjusts throughout life, as a result of the various responsibilities attained and discarded along the way. It changes as you learn and grow in leadership, like when you improve your delegation or time management skills. It also changes because your body goes through changes, that affects how much you can push yourself. For instance, during times of sickness or illness.

I was often noticed as one of those high capacity people. It was something I got praised for. I was capable of achieving a lot in a short space of time, often juggling many plates. To a degree, I am still like this. But my capacity has gone through changes and adjustments as a result of being a mother, having a husband whose job takes him across the country and beyond, and various other factors including the fact that I just don't want to live so close to my capacity line anymore.

The unique aspect of 'meeting your capacity', is this irreversible crossroad you arrive at. It's the point where you know you are forced to confront the state of your life. Where you realise, that there are limits to what you can do, how you do it and for how long. This meeting is significant enough that you know you can't keep going on as you are, and you know you can't go back to the way life was previously. Many prematurely quit when they reach this point in an effort to return to a previous way of life. It's often the first time you wonder whether you can actually continue in your role. The triggers for this meeting are:

- **Time.** "How will I ever achieve everything in the time I have?"
- **Family.** "I'm not sure I can have a healthy family and do this job"

MEETING YOUR CAPACITY

- **Sleep.** "I can't sleep! I am so tired. I don't know how long I can keep this up?"
- **Health.** The doctor tells you, "If you keep going like this, you will burnout. And it won't be easy to come back from" or "You need to go on medication."
- **Needs and demands.** "How will I ever be able to meet the needs of my people? There is so much, and I can't do everything"

Even though my final trigger for meeting my capacity happened as a result of family, I have certainly experienced a lot of the other factors at different points. In fact, for many leaders all of the above are factors at the meeting point. It's possible that you meet it more than once, I guess I haven't progressed enough into leadership to know yet. If you strategise well in response to the first meeting, I'd hope it's possible that you never have a second. But I guess I will tell you in another 20 years of ministry.

What I have noticed, is that new leaders in the first or second year of ministry are the most susceptible to the meeting point. However, I have seen signs of it with leaders when they step into a new ministry position, particularly when there is a significant increase in responsibility. I think the reason for this susceptibility for new leaders are:

- **They are often driven by zeal**
  New leaders are excited and zealous, and that's why we love them. There's nothing like the fresh perspective, of a new leader, to widen the possibilities for everyone. Unfortunately, every positive trait can also have a negative side to it. Zeal is

attractive. But zeal as an informant for decision making is very unhealthy. Zeal by nature will neglect the self, overcommit, and respond emotionally without consideration. Alternatively, good decision-making calls on wisdom, discernment, reflection, and the consideration of other responsibilities. There is only so long a leader can, or should, rely on zeal to make decisions before it becomes detrimental to overall life.

- **They feel and/or believe they have no limits**
  When everything is going great, and you are excited about what you are doing, it can feel like you are invincible. You feel like you can do everything, your words have power, you feel like you are making a difference. There's no limitations! Why would you need to consider limits, when everything is going so well? So out of naivety we apply no limits on relationships, nights out, pastoral care requests, chats, parties, church events or services. The list goes on. Now let me make this clear - God has no limitations, but we do. If God has no limitations, certainly He isn't reliant on you to do everything? Besides, limitations are good. We don't like the word 'limits', so maybe you would prefer other words: boundaries or restraint. The Bible talks about boundaries and restraint when it comes to sin. Proverbs 25:28 says:

  > *"Like a city whose walls are broken through is a person who lacks self-control."*

  In this passage, walls are significant. Walls are akin to restraint over passions, desires and the like. Showing restraint in life, is wise. God has given us natural inbuilt restraints: skin, muscles, sleep, eating and drinking. These weren't meant to be ignored, or to contain. They were meant to make us consistent and empower us, through self-regulation.

Other types of capacities

Ultimately, there are two types of capacities. There are those that are reasonably fixed, and those that have some fluidity. A better way of explaining it might be those that we:

- grow through
- those we steward

Capacity as discussed in the previous section, are the kinds that we can only steward. Our health, which would include sleep, eating, drinking is one of those capacities that we have limited choices with. We either learn to manage them, or we neglect them. On the other hand, the kind of capacities when it comes to 'growing', are qualities like:

- Compassion
- Love
- Kindness
- Grace
- Mercy
- Stress

There are probably more than those listed above. But these are a good start. Whether we care to acknowledge it or not, there are limits on our compassion. You start to realise that when you listen to people's problems all day, and have little patience for your family's problems. There are limits to the love you have for people, or at least the number of people you can love well. It's not a limit that has been put there by God, it's as a result of your own experiences, practical restraints and your degree of sacrifice. It's good to discover the limitations on your ability to love. It's only when your capacity to love is tested, that you realise you even have limits on it. An example might be, that you only act in sacrificial love for someone if they are nice to you. Or maybe you only can give love to someone if they give you something in return. Of course, this is of great concern to Jesus who instructs us to *'love your enemies'* (Matt 5:44). God intends for our love-capacity to grow, to encompass those who are unlovable, who treat us poorly, who don't meet our needs. It's only real love, when it is without condition. The same goes for our kindness-capacity, our grace-capacity and our mercy-capacity. The biggest calling we have in life, is to bear witness to the nature of God. Although there will always be the limitation of sin, we bear witness to God's' character when we seek to grow in love and kindness, and administer grace and mercy, as He does. Not being aware of those limits will cause you to miss the opportunity to grow. When you aren't aware of those limits, you're more likely to think "it's them", "it's their problem". God doesn't want us to point the finger, not when it could prevent us from maturing.

Finally, let's talk separately about stress, since it doesn't quite fit into the categories of love, grace, mercy etc. I do believe that it's possible for our capacity to handle stress to increase. Your stress levels have probably already increased many times throughout the course of your life. What you were able to handle in your

MEETING YOUR CAPACITY

first year of school, eventually increased to your high school self. And again, your capacity increased from that of a high schooler to be a worker and uni/college student. Once upon a time, some of you were only handling the stress of relationship with peers and parents. Now, for those of you to whom it applies, you have a spouse, a few kids, a career, mortgages and everything else. So, whilst life often demands you to increase your stress levels with its various changes, you can also increase it deliberately. Before I proceed, a disclaimer: If you have any kind of mental health condition, I would suggest that you talk this over with a counsellor or psychologist. Even if you don't have a mental health condition, I would suggest having a coach or mentor supervise such deliberate efforts to increase your stress management.

So much recent research demonstrates the malleability of neural pathways. Increasing your ability to manage stress, has got to do with changing often very rigid mindsets. I'm definitely not talking about simply suppressing yourself, or just foolishly striving. And I'm definitely not talking about just getting busier and trying to fit more in. Increasing your stress capacity, requires reflection, humility, accountability, self-awareness and discernment. So, I'm not going to tell you how to do it. That's simply not the purpose of this book. But I will tell you the broader areas of focus that to individually grow in, could help you increase your overall stress capacity. Here are a few:

- Personal management skills
- Learning to say no
- Being able to delegate
- Switching off and resting well

- Managing your emotions
- Not caring about what people think of you
- Understanding guilt and shame

I could keep going. I have certainly not arrived yet, but I have always seen every promotion of God as an opportunity to grow in my ability to handle stress, increase my skills and increase my faith. I have a standard response to any sign of being overwhelmed. I stop and reflect. I don't just assume that the overwhelming is just because I am busy. Lots of people are busy. Lots of people are busier than me. But not everyone is stressed. What's the difference between them and me? It's what they've learnt, how they perceive their situation and how they exercise discernment in resolving the matters. So, I dig deep. I reflect, prayerfully consider and I usually resort to good planning.

Being able to discern when a situation is a growth opportunity, or an exit opportunity is one of the hardest challenges to resolve. There are times, when a situation is a trigger that it's time to move on, and continued exposure to that stimuli, whether situation or person, is just going to be damaging to your long-term health and leadership. There are other times, when a situation is an opportunity to learn something new, and grow in your stress capacity. Nobody can really make that judgement for you. During the most stressful period of ministry, I couldn't walk into church on a Sunday without running to the bathroom and being physically ill. I would constantly cry at almost nothing. I was motionless at home, often sitting in my chair for hours at a time. Then I had a dream that changed everything for me, and I knew that the time had come for me to leave. If God doesn't speak to you that way, it may be worthwhile listing your non-negotiables. Those areas that would be a deal breaker for you. Offer that list to God and seek wise counsel. I believe He will honour you for exercising such wisdom.

Why does it happen?
Why do leaders meet their capacity? Here are a few reasons:

- **Capacity is praised**
  We are a very achievement-focused society. As a result, everybody is trying to fit more, into less time. Most people I know have got multiple degrees, are on fitness programs, are trying to climb the career ladder, and raise thriving children, have happy marriages, travel to Tuscany, contribute to volunteer causes, and still be sane. We all want to increase how much we read, listen to podcasts, stay current with world events...When you add it all up it's A LOT. For some of us, we are still scratching our heads trying to figure out how we can juggle it all. So, when someone comes along and says they have worked it out, we all say something to the effect of "How do you manage to do it ALL?" The underlying meaning in that question is the fact that we still think it's possible for ALL to be HAD. The fact is that we praise capacity. If someone is able to achieve a lot, we want to know how so that we can do it too. We presume that being able to do more, will make us content. The church is no different:

    - **Our programs and activities**
      In church, we can act like being able to do more,

will make everything better. If we just do more of that, more people would get saved. If we just did more of this, more people would volunteer. More people would reach out. More people would tithe. More people would invite others to their connect group. More would help in kid's ministry. If only we could do more, more, MORE! The alternative is not necessarily less. But if we aren't careful, the focus of ministry can become an answer to the question: "How much can we fit in?"

- **Our people**
We unknowingly encourage our people to live busy lives. A lot of the time, they don't need motivation; most people already have busy lives. But then we come along with our many ministry opportunities. It's not wrong that we have ministry opportunities, it's just that we sometimes plug our latest ministry ventures as though it will answer every deep seeded need to ever have existed in the human condition.

   Another way we can project the 'more' message onto our people, is how we incessantly want more people in our church. Ok, just relax. I am not against growth. The problem is that we often have little, by way of infrastructure, that would support the kind of growth we are praying for. Drawing a crowd is not the point of ministry. Jesus himself could draw a crowd, but few of them were there when it really mattered. We are meant to be discipling people, which means getting people to church is only a portion of the activity.

We also seem to be satisfied with our growth being simply sheep transference. In other words, we celebrate growth, but sometimes the growth is not a reflection of the impact we are making in the local community whereby people receive Christ for the first time. It's just Christians changing churches. In other words, we want 'more' so much that we don't seem to consider the nature of the 'more' we are getting.

☐ **We equate more activity with increased effectiveness**
I've occasionally heard a pastor say, "Work smarter, not harder". But I haven't seen a lot of pastors and leaders actually work that way. Because deep down, we think that busyness is momentum and activity is effectiveness. There was probably a time, probably in my Dad's generation, where effectiveness and success was measured in loyalty. I think that's where this idea of being the first to arrive and the last to leave, or working long hours being the evidence of effectiveness, came from. It's also because, organisations are notoriously poor at real accountability, so all we have to measure the effectiveness of an employee is their hours, the only visible and obvious measure. Never mind that they are achieving a quarter of the output that a leader who works part time might be achieving. Or the fact, that some of their long hours are because of hours of unproductive time in their allocated work time. Consider

measuring effectiveness in the reverse. When a person is genuinely smart, they should be able to work out ways to do their job within the required time. I adopted this line of thinking after I met my own capacity. Maybe I need to restructure, change or modify certain aspects of what I am doing, or who does it. But I consider it inefficient and ineffective of myself to need to be 'busy' to be effective.

Also, don't reduce your leadership, to a set of tasks. Effectiveness is not only about how much you get done. It's also about your influence. Being 'busy' doesn't at all mean you are leading well, or heading in the right direction. Even though, every church should determine what effectiveness looks like by way of their vision and mission, the overall commonality of effectiveness is the ability to move in the desired direction. If you're just busy, and nothing is moving in the desired direction...you ain't effective. Figure out where you are going, lest you go nowhere!

- **Blurred boundary lines in our roles**
David Allen talks about this in "Getting Things Done"9. Some of the confusion these days, is that job roles have changed so much. The tasks employed to do your job successfully were clearer and usually had some kind of physical output that would leave you feeling satisfied. I'd say the construction field gets it. When you look at a building that you've built, you can see it. It's tangible. These days, it's hard to know when you are being successful. I suppose this is why it is easy to gravitate toward numbers being the epitome of success. You can see it. On the other hand, how do you know if you are building a youth

ministry qualitatively? It's so internal and can be subjective. How do you know if you've finished? It sometimes feels like it could never be finished. Even if we grow, we can grow more. Even if we are supposed to disciple people, there are always more people to disciple. So often there aren't any limitations on our activities. It is an awful feeling to have little satisfaction and have a minimal sense of completion, especially when you know that the next day will generally hold the same uninviting reality. When there is a low sense of completion, you can continue to chase and chase and chase your tail, until you hit your capacity or hopefully some sense of satisfaction. We all want to feel like our work has value, that it is actually making a difference of some sort. But the blurred lines make it necessary to make our own boundaries, where once upon a time the inherent components of a role would have provided a natural boundary for us. Since, the normal practice is NOT to have boundaries, and we certainly don't teach new zealous leaders about them, we continue to perform roles without barriers. Meeting our capacity acts as the boundary we failed to intentionally make.

☐ **Spirit vs Body**

As a young adult, I thought I understood the verse in Matthew 26:41 that says *"Keep, watch and pray so that you will not give into temptation. The Spirit is willing, but the body is weak"*. It seems ridiculous now, but I fully believed that the verse was talking about the fact that the body prohibits the activity of the spirit. In other words, the spirit and body are in conflict with each other. God wants to do more, but I am stopping Him because of my physicality. To release the power of the spirit, I had to ignore my body's signals and simply 'rely on God'. I know, I'm embarrassed to divulge such nonsense. As an adult, I now realise that this verse is primarily about sin. And the bodies susceptibility to fall into temptation. It doesn't pertain to the ability to bypass the natural limitations God has inherently designed into our bodies. I would argue that ignoring the responses of the body, lowers the resistance to temptation. I know all too often how sleeplessness can reduce the heart and mind's ability to say no to the delicacies of the world. The enemy knew that by fasting, Jesus would be more vulnerable when he encouraged Him to use His power to make bread. Physical weakness distorts your perception. Ignoring the physical body's needs for sleep, food and water, is not wise.

God safely allows it

There's a great book written by Terry B. Walling, called "Stuck!"[10]. The book talks about the concept of transition. It suggests all leaders go through transitions that are influenced by a move, a conflict, changes in family life, a role change and anything else that changes the fundamental ways in which you do life. Walling suggests that transitions are opportunities to grow and develop, and sometimes leaders can be stuck in a transition unable to move forward to the uncertain future and unable to return to the past. Transitions are helpful. They help refine a leader. They give leaders an opportunity to reflect more deeply on their values and purpose. We don't like being in transitions, but they provide a great atmosphere for character to be developed and our activities to be focused. How gracious and merciful of God. How so, you ask? God wants us to last in ministry. He wants us to be invested long enough, to grow and make a difference in His church. Church by nature, is a long-term activity. To really disciple our people well, to really create cultural change in a community, we have to be in it for more than a few years. In His wisdom, He knows that we need to learn how to sustain ourselves. Long term sustainability can't be achieved by the adrenaline induced sprint we often adopt in the beginning phases of ministry. If that wasn't enough, here are a few more reasons God may allow it:

- **He is trying to teach you to focus**
The best way to focus in your budgetary spending, is to reduce how much money you have to play with. When you have less team members, you'll zero in on the critical activities to engage in. The same goes for capacity. When you realise that you don't have as much capacity as you thought, you'll start to think about how to focus the capacity you do have. You have way more chance at being successful in anything when you focus. Some of the most successful companies in the world, are the ones that decided to focus on only a few products or one core feature of their business that no one else had. They aren't doing everything. Watch Chef Gordon Ramsay when he comes into a failing restaurant, with the intention of turning it around. He often strips away their menu, and gets them to focus on making just a few, or even just one meal option and cooking it really well. That's the power of

focus. Even Jesus had very little by way of goals, in coming to earth. He developed leaders, taught, healed, and died on the cross. Obviously within that was a plethora of layers that He achieved. But His big-ticket items were to establish the leadership, teach and die on the cross. His entire three years of ministry was summed up in that.

- **He is trying to get you to employ better strategies**
We don't always live life wisely. Nor do we do ministry wisely. We are often so distracted, running on empty, missing meals or eating meals that are terribly unhealthy. We are trying to be everywhere.

A lot of the time, the things we are doing aren't really critical to the calling. We have a lot of time wasters. And surprisingly we don't ask a lot of questions about how to change that. I found myself painfully aware of this when I first entered ministry. When I worked in the airline industry, it was in the manufacturing division. People who've never worked in manufacturing don't realise that there is an intricate philosophy that exists to increase productivity through eliminating wasteful process steps or activities that don't add value to an overall process. It's called Lean (and is often referred to with other concepts like Six Sigma or 'Lean Six Sigma'). If you can refine a process by even two seconds, a process that is done millions of times a day, equates to two,million seconds. If two seconds usually costs the business twenty cents, you've just saved the business $400,000. Of course, these are ridiculous figures that I've made up. Some of my old work colleagues will probably cringe at my rudimentary example, but I am using it to prove a point. That two seconds was a time waster, and it didn't seem like a lot when you were looking at just the two seconds. But when you look at it in the big scheme of things, it's incredibly valuable. So, what's the point? What are your time and energy wasters and what are they costing you? Because if you had a good think about it, you might find that there is room to employ better strategies in how you work.

God wants you to stop reacting

I am a massive advocate of planning. When I worked in construction, it was all they ever talked about. Good risk management relied on good planning. Good communication relied on good planning. Good quality buildings that delivered on time relied on good planning. I can't see why a church can't have the entire year planned out before that year begins. Good planning means you get more time to consider. It means you can engage some of that lateral thinking and the big picture thinkers. You can have goals about where you want to be as a church in a year's time, and you can isolate the specific objectives you are going to implement to make that happen. There are times when God changes the direction, but largely I can't see why it can't be achieved. I did! In Connect Groups, I could give our leaders the dates of all meetings a year in advance.

There are some aspects of church life where you don't have a choice but to react. When a person passes away, someone is diagnosed with cancer, a conflict brews that threatens the stability of the church. But having good plans, that can be changed means that it allows for those occasions that require an immediate response.

Reacting is not a sin of course, but it can be counterproductive to the whole faith journey. If we only ever come to God when life is going bad, you're probably not fully experiencing the beauty of a God-relationship. Plus, there is the 'putting out fires' kind of lifestyle that is just exhausting. I've worked in other workplaces like that and it's awful. How do you ever feel like you are getting somewhere when you are constantly putting out fires? It's the equivalent to living from week to week and having no way of planning for those extra big bills or a holiday. The fact is, fires start from the same components. So, if we know that, why are we unable to prepare for them? I know I am talking quite conceptually about something that involves people who don't abide by a concept. But imagine what sort of difference it would make to our churches, if instead of putting out fires we had leadership development happening from a young age? What kind of believers would we be creating?

Worst case scenarios

So, what can actually happen if we don't take the invitation to learn how to manage our fixed capacities well?

Burnout

It's really critical that we talk about burnout for a second. I'm not going to use any illustration or analogy to get this point across. Because I trust that you will listen, because it is important, not because I convinced you with linguistic arts. It's possible that you, the reader, are a new leader. I want to warn you that other leaders, may suggest that burnout is not a real thing.

Much to the dismay of every General Practitioner and

Psychologist in the Western World. They may tell you that burnout is not real or a symptom of not relying on God. I would like to offer you an alternative viewpoint for your consideration. Overworking is more of a sign of a failure to rely on God. Why would we need to do so much, if we trust that Jesus will build HIS church? The fact is real burnout is medically evidenced through observable measures. It's not a whimsical, fantastical notion, overly conceptualised, subjective experience. It can be seen and measured. The greatest evidence of the reality of burnout is the Japanese concept of Karoshi translated as 'death from overwork'. It is a terrible concept that whilst continues to be officially unrecognised by the Japanese government and major corporations, compensation has been given for up to 400 cases per year. The estimate is approximately 10,000 deaths per year in relation to Karoshi.[11] The phenomenon is characterised by sudden death, often as a result of stroke or heart attack, with no other explainable reason. It also includes suicide in relation to work. In the cause of death analysis, pre-existing health conditions and pre-existing mental health issues are ruled out. Individual cases can be found in major newspapers like the Japan Times, Business Insider and the New York Times. In 2017, a 31 year old reporter suddenly died from a heart attack. There was no evidence of any other factors at play, besides a work pattern of 150 hours in overtime in one month. That's a total of 310 hours in a month, or close to 80 hours per week for a month. A 31 year old!! This isn't a person who has worked for 40 years, are physically decaying and are grossly fatigued. They don't have four children and are trying to study and build a career. She was only working. This could be anyone of us, or anyone of our young leaders who trust us and model our behaviour. I've read cases of 27 year old's dying on account of Karoshi. This kind of workaholism relates more to idolatry than service.

With regard to 'not relying on God' as a causal factor for burnout, I have been unable to find any undeniable suggestion in scripture that burnout relates to our beliefs and doctrine, or trust in God. I'm not implying that there are components of burnout that are unspiritual. I am simply saying that I have not seen a singular spiritual factor, like 'not relying on God', as the only component of burnout. It is negligent of leaders, to draw superbly unproven conclusions about burnout. If Christian leaders are wrong about it, the consequences of their error is dire. And what is the agenda for over-spiritualising such a risky concept? I can't think of a single positive agenda for such suggestions. Be careful of another Christian's desire to over-spiritualise significant matters like burnout.

The church society is all too quick to label stress as burnout. Feeling exhausted, tired or stressed is not necessarily burnout. Burnout has persistent physical symptoms that often a doctor can isolate. So, we shouldn't necessarily freak out at the first sign of stress or pressure. But let's not be ignorant about burnout either. We are meant to steward this body that we have been given. Care for it and nurture it. This is what sustainability is all about. I would encourage you as the next generation of leaders to fight the good fight. Bring the kingdom principles to earth in this regard. Model success in ministry, with the absence of obsession. Go against the pattern of this world. Resist the temptation for your identity to be vested in your work. Let's be the witness to the world of true contentment in life, rather than man-made striving.

Family

For some of you, this section may not be relevant...yet. But I think it warrants some extra attention for those of you to whom it applies. I'm not 100% sure why Paul suggested that it is better to stay single in 1 Corinthians 7. But I know that it is complicated to be in ministry, particularly the way it exists these days, and have a full thriving family. If we aren't careful, family becomes secondary to everything. It's not impossible though. The way Timothy talks about the responsibilities of a leader, in the New Testament, appear to represent the health of your family as intertwined with ministry. These days we tend to compartmentalise ministry and family, but the way it's written suggest that you can't even really consider yourself 'successful' in leading, if your family are in disarray. Timothy doesn't compartmentalise. He assumes a consistency of servitude and love toward our followers and our family.

The reason our families need to be specifically addressed in this chapter, is because when you have a family your capacity is no longer determined by only your ability to achieve. If your family aren't being factored into your capacity, then you're in a really risky place. Your family also has a capacity. Your spouse has a capacity for how long they are able to handle your absence, whether physically or mentally. Your children have a capacity for how long they are able to handle you helping everyone else but them. Only you can be a mother or a father to them. You are irreplaceable to them. And you can't reverse time if you get it wrong. Be aware of their capacity. My daughter is now six years old and she usually can't handle me being out more than two nights a week. She has already shown significant signs of being a quality time person, and is devastated if 'Family Day' on

Saturday gets blown out by something. So, I am naturally very protective of that day. Sometimes when you are in ministry, and your family members aren't, you can be tempted to expect them to be understanding of the weight that you carry. This translates to expecting them to make consolation for you when you aren't able to be the parent or spouse that you are called to be. But I would caution against this. You aren't a victim. You've chosen to do ministry, for which they are often suffering. Don't expect favours from them, it's likely that you are getting way more out of this calling than they are. The calling to ministry, isn't to serving the church with the exclusion of your family. You serve the church best, when you are serving your family… it's part and parcel of the calling.

Depression
This is obviously a massive issue across the board for society. But people are often shocked to realise how significant it is amongst Christian leaders. I wouldn't have predicted it was such a problem for my colleagues when I first started working in a church. In fact, I couldn't understand how it could happen. Aren't churches supposed to be life-giving?

I finally understood when it started to happen to me too. I can't even really isolate exactly when it started. But I suppose there were a few factors that were happening at the same time. I was feeling fairly disillusioned. I was certainly discouraged. After three years, I didn't really feel like I had grown or the area I was leading had grown. I felt flat. There was a sense of monotony I began to experience with my work. I felt pretty hopeless about making a real difference through my ministry. I started to lose confidence in myself, and I asked questions that were persistently unanswered: 'Why am I here? Does anything ever really change?'

For others, the path to depression is different. I don't know if there is any solution I can offer, besides the encouragement to see someone. In the year after a change in leadership, I saw a counsellor six times. I'm not ashamed to say it. I felt like I was constantly working through stuff that year. And I would do it again, if it meant that I came out of that period without any baggage. Face pain head on. It's not the culture of our times to do that, but it is evident in the scriptures.

Pain is awful, but you can either pretend it's not there and watch it rear its ugly head frequently throughout life or you can deal with it. The positive side of dealing with it is that you can have confidence that it doesn't lay dormant and reappear. And you know that dealing with it, will only last for a short season and you will grow stronger and more mature. I usually assume that pain, at its climax, will last around three months. That is just a timeframe I give myself, because I know I can handle three months of working through it. Obviously there are some pains like marriage breakdown that will require longer than that.

Oppression vs Empowerment

There is this hilarious Seinfeld[12] episode, where the eccentric character Kramer decides to reverse the peephole on his apartment door. The logic is, that he will be able to see if someone is in his apartment before he goes in avoiding an intruder from beating him with a sack of pennies. Sounds fair enough. He is completely aware that people will be able to see into his own apartment, but presumes that the only reason they would want to, is to cop a glimpse of his physique. Which he is apparently OK with. Of course, you could probably imagine the adventures that entail. In one scene, the property manager is trying to track him down. Kramer's instinct is to run and hide, but of course, the manager can see everything he is doing through the reverse peephole!

Have you ever looked through the reverse side of a peephole? You can actually still see something on the other side, even if it's difficult to make out. It's because of a special type of lens. It's so fascinating to me that the side of the door you are standing on, effects what you see.

That's how I would describe the difference between oppression and empowerment. Sometimes, the areas we lead feel weighty and hard to handle. Sometimes we take it in our stride and proactively steer and make choices. I call the first oppression, and the second empowerment. Oppression is negative. It is heavy, bears down and restricts your movement. Whilst empowerment on the other hand is freeing. Empowerment gives hope, finds a way, because you realise that you have the authority and autonomy to decide. So, what accounts for those moments when you feel oppressed versus empowered? Perspective. The side of the door you stand on, determines whether you feel oppressed or empowered.

Despite what we think, God operates in the realm of empowerment. Even though He wants us to be submitted and surrendered, and do His will…the choice is still ours to be submitted, surrendered and do His will. We are empowered to obey. We have grace, that sustains us to keep trying, because our failings no longer have the final say. On the other hand, oppression is the opposite to what God wants us to experience. Oppression is what Jesus was offering freedom from when He said, *"Come to me, all you who are heavy burdened...*" (Matt 11:28) The additional laws and rules posed by the Pharisees were oppressive.

So why would we ever feel oppressed by what we have before us? The specific perspective that determines whether we feel oppressed or empowered, is whether we believe we have to 'carry' burdens. When you carry responsibility, you feel like everything rests on your shoulders. You feel alone. Isolated. You feel like you are the only one. And sometimes you look around at the people you lead, and you could be justified in this belief. This feeling is like oppression. It bears down on you, restricting your movement and choices. "What can I do?" is the typical statement in the oppression perspective. You feel so constrained. The reality is, no matter how much the situation can look and feel oppressive, you always have the Holy Spirit. That may not seem like enough sometimes, but the Bible promises that the Holy Spirit is actually all we need to live this life, including its various responsibilities. Including ministry.

Empowerment on the other hand is when you know you aren't enough, but that God has got your back. It's His ministry anyway, and He's going to bring His will to pass. You might not have the answers, but He does.

> **Empowerment is when you know you aren't enough, but that God has got your back**

I often find leaders will start a year feeling empowered, but as they fatigue the responsibilities feel more like oppression. The important idea to remember is that perspective makes all the difference. If you are seeing the world from the corridor looking into the warm cosy home, the image you see is going to be unclear and unhelpful. If you are seeing the world from within the warm cosy home looking out into the corridor, ministry actions will be a lot clearer. And what's better is that you'll be able to prepare more effectively for whatever is at your door.

What do we do about it?
So, what can you do if you find yourself meeting your capacity?

- **Be willing to ask the hard questions**
  We often don't like asking the hard questions, because they have the ability to shake our foundations. But they are necessary,. Here are a few questions that are worth asking when you meet your capacity:

    o Is this really what God wants me to do?
    o Am I carrying burdens rather than managing responsibilities?
    o Am I focused? Am I getting involved in unnecessary politics? Am I working the smartest way? Can I engage someone who works smarter, to show me how to do it well? Is this an opportunity to work as a team?
    o What is worth my time? What tasks don't require someone with my specific skill set?
    o What aspects cause me to feel overwhelmed? What is my recovery plan?
    o What am I disappointed with? Am I feeling discouraged? Who can I talk to about that?
    o Should I get a coach or a mentor?

MEETING YOUR CAPACITY

☐ **Assess your general percentage of operation**
The problem with running at your capacity, is that it doesn't plan or prepare well for those life circumstances that are out of your control. Your kids getting sick. An injury. A financial emergency. Running at your capacity doesn't leave any room or buffer for a change or interruption. Imagine, having a full glass of water on the edge of a table. When that water is at the absolute brim, it doesn't take a lot for the water to spill. Something could shake the floor. Someone could bump the table. However, if that glass of water is 60% full, it's a totally different scenario. The same occurrences don't affect the water. It's in our best interest to live at a reasonable operational percentage. I suggest you assess your glass of water. Where are you on that scale? Are you at 90% or 75%? For some of you, with the complexity of e.g. multiple children, health issues in your lives even 75% is too high. Think about your busiest times of the year…where are you then? If you have to sustain between 85-100% for 2-3 months, you are in the danger zone.

One more thing, if there is an earthquake, it doesn't matter how full that glass of water is, it's more than likely to spill. Don't be too hard on yourself if a major life change puts you on the side lines for a while. Your glass of water had no hope. Don't believe Instagram, everybody's glass would have spilled in the same circumstances. A marriage breakdown, a death, job loss…these are major life changes. Being kind to yourself, is also about knowing when to stop and when to rebuild.

- **Manage and adjust expectations**

  We probably don't regularly assess this, but our tasks, responsibilities or demands are quite fluid. They generally don't stay the same. Sometimes you need to be more invested in your kid's life, because they could be facing challenges. But the rest of the time, its business as usual. When you have a major event that you are critical in organising, it requires more of you than after the event. That's just common sense. Strangely, we tend to keep our expectations fairly rigid despite the fact that everything else is in perpetual motion. I'm not talking about values. Our values shouldn't change. But our expectations are not always based on values, nor are they always a truthful reflection of life. An example might be "I'm not a good mother, if my home is untidy". That's probably not a truthful statement. It's helpful if a mum is tidy, but it doesn't necessarily translate to good parenting. Another might be, "I have to be there. I'm not a good pastor if I'm not there for people". Well actually a lot of the time you don't need to be there. I can't imagine Andy Stanley, Senior Pastor of North Point Church, being at every major life event of the members of his megachurch. Hence, our expectations can be fairly detrimental, if we are applying a rigid belief to a malleable situation. We can actually manage our expectations. We can adjust them based on the seasons we are in. If you have a major event coming up, why not have a moment to consider what expectations you normally have of yourself and whether you can temporarily adjust them for the season you are in? Why not adjust certain work expectations? I've listened to so many people over the years complain about not being able to do everything when things get busy. They panic, they start putting requests in for more staff. I'm not saying this response is bad. But sometimes it would be helpful just to stop and consider what expectations could be adjusted.

When it comes to my compassion-capacity, I have a bit of a rule with myself. Often I would have pastoral catch-ups in the afternoon. So, when I would have a really heavy pastoral care meeting that might have rattled me, I would call it a day. That was my way of saying "Yep! That's probably all I can take today. That's the limit." I wouldn't try and push it. I would recognise, that my capacity to do good work after hitting my compassion limit was probably not going to be valuable time anyway. Usually on the drive home, I would be yelling at the enemy, and praising God too. When you are generally organised, you know you can do that.

☐ **Don't compare**
In life, this is generally a good idea! But with regard to leadership, there is no greater capacity killer. You have your lane, and they have theirs. You aren't meant to do what they are doing. Comparison is just silly anyway, because every leader is a unique individual with their own set of circumstances. How could you even begin to accurately compare yourself to someone who has so many variables different to you? It's the classic comparing oranges with apples scenario. Nobody is the same. We aren't meant to be. The beauty of the Body of Christ, as 1 Corinthians describes is that no part is really the same. Even the similar parts aren't the same, the left foot and right foot still have differences. And yet every part is needed.

There will be some people who have a greater capacity than you, naturally because of circumstances. Just accept it. You don't need to be the same, even if everyone around you praises them. You aren't supposed to be doing this for the praise of people anyway. Stay FOCUSED. Don't be blown by the wind.

- **Sleep and Rest**

    It seems common sense, but make sure you make space for rest. Particularly when you meet your capacity. Before you start trying to make plans or engage a solution, just try resting or sleeping. This is something that I am atrocious at. Now that I am off work I have a 30 minute nap most afternoons. I struggle to rest, but I know how important it is. Unfortunately, my daughter shares the same struggle with me. She is painful to wind down for sleep. As a mum, you learn all the important stuff about sleep. It literally makes you smarter, allows for brain development, improves your body's functioning.

    Sleep is restorative. There is no way we can avoid that. Just like your stomach takes time to digest food, your brain needs to digest the day. The consequence of a lack of sleep and rest are devastating. The mining and airline industries have all been very invested in the results of various studies relating to sleep deprivation. Apparently research has suggested that staying awake for more than 24 hours leads to reduced hand eye coordination that is similar to having a blood alcohol content of 0.1%. Lacking sleep causes reduced alertness, shorter attention span, reduced decision-making skills, poor memory and reduced concentration. So, prioritise this incredible gift that God has given mankind.

MEETING YOUR CAPACITY

☐ **Account for what you can do and create some boundaries for yourself**

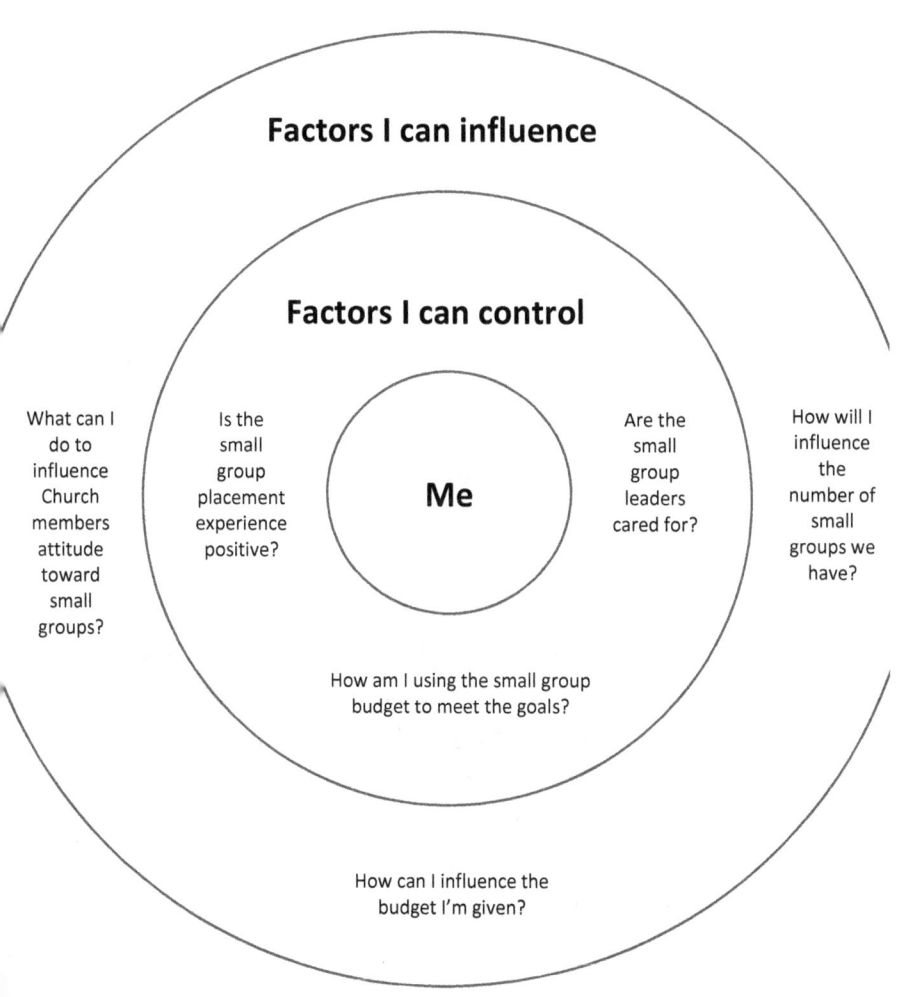

The above diagram is an example of how I take stock of the components I can really control in my life. Sometimes in my head and my heart, I have started to concern myself with situations that were never mine to manage. At best I can influence them, but I can't change them myself. It has usually been times when I am frustrated or overwhelmed that I have most used this. Oftentimes, you are frustrated and overwhelmed, and don't have any real idea as to why or how it happened. Because busyness doesn't always mean you will be overwhelmed. It can sometimes be that you are taking responsibility for situations that aren't yours to take. After I have done this, I generally make a plan of how I am going to make boundaries to prevent myself from getting dragged into the situations I can only influence.

- **Learn what you can leave until another day**
Not everything must be done on the day. Sometimes when you feel stressed, you lose the capacity to use sound decision making and it feels like you have to finish everything. It's clearly not true. Oftentimes, it would be better to leave some tasks for when you aren't stressed, and are able to think clearly. The fact is, that you would be better off using the last ten minutes of the day to work out what tasks you can allocate to another day. Instead of allowing emotions to rule your precious time and energy. Go home and be with your families, or friends, or pets. Being diligent is way more effective than that adrenaline fuelled work frenzy that makes you think you have to stay until it's dark.

MEETING YOUR CAPACITY

☐ **Make room for spontaneous play**
One of the things I regret that I didn't understand when I was working in ministry, is the value of spontaneous play. I actually learnt this from observing my now six year old daughter. Sometimes we have been guilty of using family time to go here, or go there. But I've noticed that what she really likes is time at home that's uninterrupted. She makes all sorts of strange games, and activities. She is more rested and more satisfied when she has that. So, I don't overschedule her time, particularly on holidays. She has plenty of time to just create. My parents did the same with us. I remember school holidays were rarely programmed. My mum would be doing cleaning and housework, and I would be writing, drawing, playing music, walking the dog. Whatever I felt like at the time. It was spontaneous play. I recall that I basically learnt how to play the guitar over a two month holiday. No doubt the fact that my mum had not organised events or activities, allowed me that focused time. Of course, not every kid is the same, so this isn't meant to be parenting advice. But you can look into it if you want. I was so intrigued by this discovery, that I started to research it for adults. The same applies to the grown-ups. Weekends or holidays when you don't schedule your time, can be rather relaxing. Sometimes we schedule ourselves so tightly, that we don't necessarily allow time to be spontaneous. Now I think that's a bit sad. Spontaneity is good for the heart and mind. Those days when you don't have anything planned can be the most relaxing. So as a family we have lots of time for that spontaneity. My husband Josh is ridiculously busy these days. But I've noticed that on those days that we have

nothing planned, he gets to do that which recharges him. He is also way more engaged in playing with our daughter. He does it because he wants to, not because he has to.

- **Stay close to God**
  Of course, this is a given. Continue to cultivate that relationship with God. Particularly, honesty about your situation. God doesn't want you to get burnt out, and He doesn't want your family to fall apart. Make sure you tell Him when you are worried about those things, and ask Him to send red flags when He can see it's time to do something. I was really concerned about my burn out levels at a particular time, and I had decided that I couldn't necessarily depend on the people around me to do something about it. I prayed this really significant prayer, which I can still remember. I told God that I would be trusting Him to send me a really clear message when it was time to stop. I was still working in two departments and it was slowly killing me. So, at the time, when I say stop, I was meaning finishing up with Creative. About six months later, I had a dream that was very clear to me that if I kept going I would burn out and that it was time to stop. After some conversations with the Senior Pastor, it was probably about a month or two later that I finished with Creative and was focused on Connect Groups only.

- **See a counsellor or psychologist**
  If you've hit your capacity hard, this one is a no brainer. Get some help immediately. Another situation to engage with a counsellor is when you know, or think, there is an underlying

belief that is prohibiting you from slowing down. If neither of these apply, but your family and friends seem to be giving you the same message. 'Why are you doing so much?' 'We never hang out anymore', 'We miss you', 'You don't spend any time with me' It's probably time to see a counsellor. They can't all be wrong! Maybe there's an underlying belief that you're not good enough. Maybe it's that you can't handle the idea of not being approved of and so have to keep busy to maintain the praise. Whatever it is, it is imperative that you uncover that and grow stronger. Jesus says in Matthew 16:26, *"And what do you benefit if you gain the whole world but lose your own soul? Is anything worth more than your soul?"* (NLT) Seek help! There are counsellors and psychologists who specialise in ministry. They understand all too well the mindsets that can pervade. Let someone help you.

Final thoughts...

Ministry is hard, but we can also make it unnecessarily hard for the wrong reasons. Sometimes it's us, and our brokenness that make it more difficult than it needs to be. Underlying my drivenness, was a deep desire to feel significant. For some it will be approval. For others it's comfort.

The desire for significance has permeated my life for as long as I can remember. I wanted to be a famous musician. I would constantly think about what I could do to make my mark on this world. I wanted to feel important, because truthfully I never did. So, I busied myself and worked so hard, sacrificed, tried to make myself like a well-oiled machine, because it made me feel like a somebody when I achieved goals. I actually thought God was thinking the same thing of me too! Funny how we can project our own attitudes onto God. I thought that was what He wanted. That's faithfulness right? Hitting milestone after milestone. I think even deeper down, I believed He needed me. Who will do it, if I don't? At some point, when I hit my capacity I came to realise that God is more active than I am. He is busy! He is doing a million different activities at once, He is speaking to millions of people at the same time. He is perfectly orchestrating details that I have no awareness of. And He doesn't tire. He is on a whole different level to us. He doesn't really need me. But He does want me. He wants to share the job of bringing redemption to the earth, because He is the ULTIMATE team player. Success to God isn't just an isolated individual sport of ticking off accolades, it's having a great team that works together to achieve the goals He sets. He loves it when His kids play together…just like we do. If we weren't so busy building our individual trophy cabinets, we'd see that teamwork means we don't have to meet our capacity. We have a chance to see the beauty of God, through the activation of His people and the unique gifts He has given them. Imagine what collective capacity looks like? We would be able to extend the distance we can run, with less individual effort, not because we are lazy of course, but because we can celebrate success together. Imagine if instead of individual resumes, you had team resumes…Wow. That would be cool. We wouldn't have to reach our capacity if we modelled and created great teams instead of always looking for and praising the individual player's.

The Jesus factor

You might think that there was no way Jesus could have reached a meeting point with His capacity. That we are on our own on this one. Well, you'd be wrong. Jesus met His capacity two times to my knowledge. The obvious one is when He was in the garden of Gethsemane, and He asked God to take the cup (Matthew 26:39). Jesus didn't want to go through the pain. Of course, He still obeys. But He certainly doesn't suggest that He was excited to go through with it. What the passage does suggest is that He wanted to do the Father's will. Obedience led Him to the cross. He met His capacity line, but He endured suffering, which DID kill him...for us.

The second time was when He was carrying the cross. We know that those who were crucified were required to carry their own cross. But in three of the gospels Simon of Cyrene (Matt 27:32, Mark 15:21, Luke 23:26) takes part of the job of carrying the cross to Golgotha. Jesus was heavily beaten. He was repeatedly struck on the head. He was flogged with a whip that was made of leather with pieces of bone and shards of pottery in it. It was not uncommon for some victims not to survive the Roman flogging, let alone carry a cross to be crucified. It's not really a surprise that Simon had to assist Him in carrying the cross. Jesus had a physical limit too, just like us. Yes, He had a crazy pain threshold, but He still couldn't do it all. He couldn't endure such a painful beating and carry the cross. And since the cross was the final part of the plot...God provides Him with Simon to share the load. So, He could make it to Golgotha and finish it all.

So, what do we learn? Don't feel ashamed that you have a capacity, because we have a saviour who can empathise. You don't need to be a hero for the sake of it, let Jesus be the hero you need. Ask God for discernment and wisdom, to know when to endure and when to change. Ask for help. Don't go it alone. Rely on a collective capacity to get it done, becoming the ultimate team player like God and don't let ministry become an individual sport.

Serve God with joy and wisdom, not in carelessness and arrogance. Because someone is always watching you. Whether it be the people you lead, or your kids. Give them a reason to have fond thoughts of ministry because of the example you set…

CHAPTER 5

Identity loss

When I was a kid I loved pretending to be a singer. I really wanted to be a professional singer, and worked toward that career for a long time. Standing in front of the mirror, with my deodorant can I would belt out some tunes, usually Mariah Carey. It's funny you know, my parents and brother never complained, although they did catch me a few times in the middle of my performances. I loved the way singing made me feel, and I imagined myself on a big stage commanding it with my big voice. I assumed that people would like me better if I was a singer too. After singing is when I would hear all the encouragement:

"You sounded just like Mariah Carey!"
"Wow, you're such a great singer, Mel!"
"You could be a professional one day"
"You could be a somebody"

Pretending to be someone is one matter. Wanting to become another person...that's a whole different story! I recently watched an old movie called "*The Talented Mr Ripley*". Tom Ripley a poor unknown, through a series of events comes to be friends with

Dickie Greenleaf, a wealthy young man travelling in Italy on his extremely wealthy father's peso. The two become great friends, and spend lots of time together, living what is really Dickie's lifestyle. Prior to befriending Dickie, Tom was really a nobody, who could play the piano superbly, but performed menial jobs and resided in a decrepit apartment in a forgotten part of New York City. Dickie is everything you would expect a son of a rich father. He doesn't have a lot of regard for people, he has rich friends, went to the finest schools, is a brat and he is used to getting what he wants. Tom becomes obsessed with Dickie, and eventually, they have an awful fight in which Tom murders Dickie. Tom, after becoming so in love with Dickie and his lifestyle decides to steal his identity, since nobody besides Tom knows of his death. It is a bone-chilling movie, with layer upon layer of deception and lies. He fakes Dickies voice, forges his signature and rents apartments under Dickie's name. He was all too used to lying, and one piled on top of another.

However, the greatest lie Tom told was the one he told himself from way back in those days of anonymity...that his life would be better if he was somebody else. His first statement in the opening of the movie is revealing:

> "If I could just go back.
> If I could just rub everything out.
> Starting with myself"[13]

Even if you don't have such self-loathing like Tom, it's possible there are times when you've thought life would be better if you had been someone else. I have. Being one of the only coloured people in my school, and often feeling like I was different, caused me to believe for decades that I would have been better off if I was a white, blond, Australian. It took me years to come to a place where I was remotely grateful for the unique way that God had packaged me.

I've discovered that any vulnerability you have in your identity is exposed in ministry. And what's more, ministry can become part of how you define yourself. If you have ever desired to be a somebody, the enemy has a way of twisting your wholesome desires for service to become a replacement for the identity you lack. It never happens suddenly, it's always a subtle entry point like some encouragement, a word or prophecy, or the special privileges you get with your role. But the outcome is leaders believing that they need to be a pastor. They can't do without it. They feel lost, if they didn't have a people to lead. The titles and positions start to matter more than they should. The meetings become a sign of importance. People listening to you makes you feel like you are worth being listened to. Ministry gives you purpose, instead of God giving you purpose. Ministry becomes our identity. We can do that with lots of the roles we play in life besides ministry. We can do that with parenthood, marriage, a relationship, a job, our financial status, and appearance. We think those roles are what makes our lives important, and to not have them would be dire. We clearly don't understand our value to God, if we think that such roles have the ability to render our lives meaningless or purposeful.

> Any vulnerability you have in your **identity** is **exposed** in ministry

What is identity?

Generally, identity has got to be one of the strangest concepts to define. The scriptures don't actually use the word identity, but there is plenty in scripture to suggest that who we think we are collectively and individually has incredible significance. It's important to note here, that whilst we are individuals and we have a personal relationship with God, the majority of what scripture talks about in reference to identity is collective. As in, it mostly refers to us, as the body of believers as opposed to me as an individual. That doesn't make it any less remarkable of course.

Identity is essentially the answer to these questions. Who are we? And therefore, who am I?

Being a habitual overthinker, I have asked myself that question a lot. How do you define the self, without personality profiles, interests, parents, heritage, gender, or even the roles you play in society? To answer that question generally relies on your self-perception. Yet at the same time identity isn't so subjective to be established by ourselves. It certainly can't rely on the person who has an agenda in defining it; we are too heavily emotionally invested in defining our identity for it to be true and accurate. Our identity isn't easily changed either, it's rather stable. I don't even think we can really say it's simply what you 'believe' you are, not in the modern sense of the word 'believe'. These days 'believe' can mean mentally and emotionally agreeing with an idea, but it doesn't necessarily translate to our life choices. It's those core beliefs that are more like subconscious conviction, deep in the inner parts of our being that rise to the surface through circumstance particularly painful ones.

Identity is actually a very difficult concept. And yet it does impact how we live. I have known of Christians who have walked away from a relationship with God because they didn't believe they identified with what they have seen it represent. People end marriages because they don't think they can be what their spouse desires. People dress according to their self-perception. They chose careers based on self-perception. They buy houses in places and drive cars that they equate with their identity. Then of course is the elaborate effort we go through to ensure that others 'identify' us the way we want to be identified. We'll try to hang around certain people, and avoid others. We curtail our personalities and topics, to hide or reveal who we think we are. We lie in word and behaviour because we are trying to protect the identity we want.

As a society, in general, we are really good at losing our identities too. We lose them in relationships. We lose them in jobs. We lose them in our political opinions. And believers are no exception to this. Religion can be an attempt to define ourselves. We can become concerned with the observable markers[14] of being a Christian, rather than having an actual relationship with God. In this scenario, the Christian identity revolves around the question: "What do Christians do?" Instead of directing their activities towards a faithful love relationship with God. Because 'good Christians' and 'faithful Christians' aren't necessarily the same concept. Sometimes, faithfully following God will make you look rather stupid and lack those behavioural markers we've culturally deemed 'Christian'. If you need an example of this examine the life of Jesus' mother, Mary. Her obedience to carry the Son of God out of wedlock, didn't look like faithfulness to the people of that time.

So, in essence, one of the biggest reasons we would lose our identity in ministry is the same as anyone else who loses their identity in any area of life. We aren't as stable in our identity as we think. And we are severely uncertain about who we are.

God and us

I had never really understood the concept of the '*I AM*' (Exodus 3:14) phrase that God uses to describe himself when he introduces Himself to Moses. Even after reading commentary after commentary. The significance of it, in the context of a discussion on identity, certainly opens up my understanding. God himself is the only One who doesn't require an explanation to define who He is. Maybe we need it, but He doesn't. He just is.

We define ourselves as human beings by comparing ourselves to someone else. Which is why I think the habit of comparison stems from uncertainty about identity. Imagine I was the only Indian in the world. Seemingly impossible to imagine…relax non-Indians. I'm allowed to say those kinds of jokes. You would identify me as 'The Indian One', because that is what makes me unique. But just imagine if every person in the world, was Indian? 'Indian' would no longer be a defining quality. Our entire definition of ourselves, rely on the context we find ourselves in. This doesn't apply to God. He is who He is, and it doesn't matter when or where He is.

Because of this, we are susceptible to identity loss or shift, because our contexts are also susceptible to change even though our subconscious conviction may not. We get married. We have kids. We get older. Even our personalities can be open to change. Not because we change them deliberately, although some do. But because the development of the self is not fully realised when you do your first, second or third personality test. The development of the self is a lifelong journey, and not everybody starts at the same place in the maturation process. Even the concept of 'identity in Christ' demonstrates the same idea. Who we are, depends on Christ's identity.

So, what's the point of all of this? Again, our identity isn't as stable as we think. And we are severely uncertain about who we are.

With our identities not being foolproof, we have a tendency to get caught up in the prevailing culture of the communities in which we find ourselves. Group behaviour is contagious. That's not necessarily negative. It's part of the reason we often have an interest in the study of culture because we recognise it can influence positive group behaviour or weed out those who don't fit that culture. If you want a new Christian to start with a solid standing in the Word, have them hang around people who are passionate about the Word. If you want someone to grow in the prophetic, put them in an environment where the majority are prophetic. If you want a person to grow in evangelism, put them amongst evangelists. It's just common sense, and biblical. People are heavily influenced by their peers.

In church leadership, there is also a prevailing culture that you either embody or you oppose. Sometimes these prevailing cultures aren't based on the most mature ideas either. Appearance can affect whether you fit in or not. Being seen as a 'troublemaker' determines if you fit in or not. On the positive side, the culture can encourage staff members to pray more, read the Word more and love more. Whether we like it or not, uniformity is often the desired condition for the groups in which we belong. And that uniformity is not always based on becoming Christ-like. Think about charisma. The scriptures tell us that there was nothing about Jesus that would have deemed him as having charisma. Authority, yes. But not charisma. But in some church's charisma is elevated to the greatest of importance. People showing the signs of it, are often promoted regardless of competency. Despite the fact that leadership literature demonstrates that the more successful leaders are those that are often the opposite to charismatic, for instance in the case of 'Good to Great' by Jim Collins[15]. The point is, if you haven't got a clear understanding of who you are, the group culture can begin to dictate to you, its desired identity. And to preserve your identity, you may be resisting group mentality.

Why should we be concerned?
Surely it's self-explanatory why it's not good to have your identity wrapped up in ministry. But one of those reasons requiring special attention, is the incessant need for validation. The need for validation arises as soon as our identity begins to attach to ministry. When ministry becomes the primary method for judging your value, you become infatuated with matters that communicate importance. Here are a few examples of the indicators of importance that you may become preoccupied with:

- Platform ministry time
- Numbers, Statistics and measures
- Position and Title
- Reserved parking spots
- Seating on a Sunday

- ☐ Money and earnings
- ☐ Name dropping
- ☐ Office size, and possibly how close it is to the boss
- ☐ Having more influence with the Senior Pastor than others

If your choices only affect yourself, then maybe it's not that big a deal. Afterall, your choices are between you and God. But when you are a leader, the majority of your decisions affect the people in your church.

So maybe you're thinking "Mel, a reserved car spot seems rather inconsequential to the people I lead or those around me?" True. But more to the point, if self-validation can affect your perspective of a carpark, what else is being influenced by self-validation? Isn't it possible that how you're treating people is not for their benefit but yours? Maybe the unhealthy work habits, that are coming painfully close to burnout, are really about validation? Maybe neglecting your family, isn't because you love ministry, maybe they are just the collateral damage in your plans for self-validation? Who knows the extent to which the need for validation will travel? We are the worst identifiers of our own personal agendas. Particularly if we stand to gain from the agenda, our subconscious finds it rather hard to look objectively.

The good news is that God is understanding, and offers true validation. In Christ, we can see our true importance and value. Both corporately and individually. Our value to Him is innate, it's not dependent on what is done or not done. There aren't signs that you have to look for as proof of your value. I could rattle off all the verses you already know: Psalm 139, Jeremiah 29:11. But the one that actually blows my mind specifically when it comes to validation, is Ephesians 2:6-7:

> *"And God raised us up with Christ and seated us with him in the heavenly realms in Christ Jesus, in order that in the coming ages he might show the incomparable riches of his grace, expressed in his kindness to us in Christ Jesus."*

We are lifted up and seated with Christ. None of which is our doing. We are honoured and showered with pride from the Father, because we are a demonstration of God's kindness. Just like the awesome imagery in Job, where God is praising Job before Satan and the angels. Like a Dad who wants to tell his co-workers what His beautiful children did or said. We are special. And we are valued so much that we get to sit with Christ. As co-heirs. How's that for validation?

Signs and symptoms

It is highly ineffective to use your feelings to gauge whether ministry has become your identity. So here is my hot list of signs and symptoms:

- **You take it very personally when someone leaves your church or ministry**

    There is a part of your response when someone leaves, that is normal. You've often spent lots of time investing in that person, and it can be a bit disappointing to feel like another church or ministry is going to benefit. It's not ideal that we feel this way, but yeah it can hurt. However, there is a time when your efforts to change a volunteer's mind, or even to express your disdain about their decision is more of a reflection of

IDENTITY LOSS

what is going on in you. People move on, it's not a sin. Yes, we should be concerned if there is a possibility that they are falling away from their faith. But a lot of the times, that's not at all the reason they are leaving. When you've lost your identity in ministry, your ministry and self, become one. Which means, when someone leaves it feels like a personal rejection, rather than what it might more innocently be: the leading of the Holy Spirit.

☐ **You determine your value based on how your ministry is represented**
There are times when your ministry gets overshadowed by another. It might be with regard to resources, or praise. Nobody intends for the overshadowing, it just happens. When your identity is lost in ministry, it can feel like you are being undervalued...even though it's not necessarily about you. The fact is, there are some ministries that do get undervalued. When I used to work in construction, the Rehabilitation Department was constantly being overshadowed by the Safety Department. It never felt like a personal attack. In fact, it used to act as motivation for me to make more 'believers'. There were all sorts of assumptions that people would deduce to explain the overshadowing...some bad, some good. But it just happens sometimes that the leader doesn't recognise equally every organisational activity. It may not be permanently like that, it may just be because they have to focus on sorting one particular area out. It might be because they are just really passionate about a particular area. Regardless of what role I find myself in, I will always advocate for Connect Groups.

And maybe that will overshadow other departments. The issue is, when you see your ministry as intimately entwined with yourself, it becomes difficult to separate something that is meant to be an objective matter from a personal subjective one.

☐ **You take it personally when you are excluded**
There are times when you aren't needed. Maybe it's a meeting, or a conference. It's not meant to be personal. In fact, usually it's because someone is trying to be a good steward of time and money. Afterall, it's good stewardship that is ensuring you get paid each week. If it really hurts though, then there is a good chance that your value is being measured by inclusion. A church is this unique convergence of workplace and church home. When decisions are made that exclude you, it's probably a 'work' decision rather than a 'my church home' decision. There are times when people deliberately exclude you. It could be someone using their power to control, manipulate or keep you at arm's length. The fact is, you would be way better equipped to deal with that, if your needs for inclusion were coming from somewhere else. Your workplace is not always the place for your needs to be met. You are there to meet needs. That doesn't mean you ignore your own needs, but you may need to consider meeting those needs in other healthy ways. Get into a Connect Group. Start playing sport. Join a book club.

☐ **You find it hard to take holidays**
It can be hard to take holidays when you are the only person

in a department. But sometimes, that should probably be your boss' issue to resolve rather than yours since they are in charge of resourcing the workplace appropriately.

> We are severely **uncertain** about who we are

Holidays and breaks are really important. They actually make you better at what you are doing. However, there are times when we refrain from taking holidays, because we are too busy. Church is always busy. Why would you base your decisions for life around church busyness, that essentially never changes? The other predicament is that you take holidays, but only when you have reached the point of complete exhaustion. You end up taking a week here or there, because basically you need the week off just to survive. Okay, it probably seems like a wise decision. But holidays aren't only about rest. They are also about refocusing and recharging. When you are exhausted and all you can do is pass out, you don't have the time to review or reflect. Reflection is pertinent to the journey of a believer. Particularly prayerful reflection. When you stop and consider, you give yourself a chance to be intentional about your choices. You can take stock of where you are with your different relationships, especially with God.

- **All you read are ministry and leadership books**
It's commonplace for leaders to read books. Often that's the main theoretical training you are getting. It also is helping you grow and refrain from becoming stale. The risk with reading only ministry or leadership books, is how it further enhances the infatuation with ministry. You go home and you're still thinking,

planning, getting ideas for your ministry. Your mind does need to switch off. In fact, it's often in those switched off moments that you have your best ideas. So let your brain regenerate, and give it a break from thinking about work by restricting the amount of leadership and ministry books you read. Often the solution to problems is not found in a book anyway. How many more books could we possibly read? Knowledge isn't always the answer.

- **You've lost interest in your interests**
Prior to ministry, you often have hobbies that you enjoy that have nothing to do with ministry. Mine was writing music. Unfortunately, when I started working in church I slowly began to forfeit that interest and my spare time was taken up with more people, more nights out, and just generally a lot of other activities that were somehow attached to ministry growth. Now it's really hard to get back into, because I don't feel the same way as I used to about it. I was always a goal setter too. I would have a list that I would write on New Year's Eve every year, and they would often have fun goals…Just because. After a while my personal goals began to diminish, with the exception of relationship with God goals, and 'ministry' goals became front and centre. Your personal goals and personal interests is part of what makes you unique. To lose such interests out of sheer busyness and ministry growth, is just a real shame. Don't lose that which makes you who you are.

- **Everything else feels like waiting**
It seems like a strange one, but sometimes when you are just going through the motions the in-between time feels

like a holding pattern until you are back at work again. Or in the case of ministry, when it's Sunday again. It can feel like the time that you are home, is akin to holding your breath. Maybe your Saturdays have become something other than an opportunity to explore outside interests. Maybe it's just become the mandatory family time that you've locked in to fulfil obligations. This is when you know that life is revolving around ministry. Everything else feels like the 'in-between'.

☐ **All you talk about is ministry**
Do you find that all of your conversation somehow ends up being about ministry? Maybe not with your congregation members. With them you might be actually trying to minister which is still 'ministry'. When your conversations with your spouse or friends are all about ministry, when your conversations with family are all about ministry, when you find it hard to talk to non-believers because you want to talk about ministry, but it makes no sense to them...it may be a sign that your identity is lost in ministry. This can often be a reason for the gravitation toward friendships with fellow ministers. You tell yourself it's because your life is so different and normal people don't understand. But actually, it's because you don't have anything else to talk about.

☐ **You're always striving for more recognition or position**
The problem with recognition and position is revealed in Philippians 2:3 *"Do nothing out of selfish ambition or vain conceit. Rather, in humility value others above yourself, not looking to your own interests but each of you to the interests of others".*

It's not wrong to ask God for a promotion. Sometimes it is time to move on. There is an unsettledness that happens in you. However, sometimes the desire for change is really the desire for a positional or status change, which can be related to self-validation. If we are being genuinely obedient to Philippians 2:3, we would be looking to promote others alongside us and underneath us. Rather than looking for ways to promote ourselves.

- **You take it personally when all isn't going well in your ministry**
It is a fact of life that ministry doesn't always go as well as you would like. So, ride the wave of good times as long as you can, whilst simultaneously preparing yourself. The hard ministry days can reveal the degree to which a person's identity has become lost in ministry. If you crumble frequently over your attendance, that's probably not fantastic. If you go into a full-blown depression when goals aren't achieved, that's not a great sign. If you assume that everything bad that is happening in your ministry, indicates that there must be something wrong with you or that you aren't a good pastor or leader, it's worth considering how your identity is being affected by ministry. Yes, as John Maxwell states: *"Everything rises and falls on leadership"*.[16] That doesn't mean that you are 100% at fault for every circumstance that arises when you are the leader. That's like assuming that parents are 100% responsible for how their kids turn out and we know that's not really true. If your worship leader ran off with a married person, how could that be your fault? If one of your key leaders decides to divide

the church because He can do a better job…that's not really on you. People sin under your leadership, and you won't ever be held responsible for that. What the famous John Maxwell quote does mean, is that you are 100% responsible for doing something about it. You may not have asked for the specific circumstances you find yourself in, but be the leader and take action when it does. The only point in which you are at fault, is when you lie down and wash your hands clean of responsibility. To make a personal judgement on yourself, is to doubt God's wisdom to call you. Don't wallow in the gutter of inactivity, that's not where you belong. Find that warrior spirit that fights for your people, and get up. Humbly pray, and make a plan. Don't let the hard times become your measure for your call.

- **You take credit when things are going well**
Things go well sometimes, and again they aren't always 100% because of you. Sometimes God just gives you unbelievable favour, and everything you touch turns to gold. Be careful that you don't assume that there is something special about you, which brings about such success. Sometimes it was your idea, and it was your influence. Great! Be grateful to God for the success you together brought to pass. It is questionable when you have to announce your part to the world. They don't need to know. You know and God knows. Telling the world, is probably a good sign that you are seeking recognition, praise or validation. Or you just love yourself a little too much.

When you are desperate for validation, you begin to take credit for successes that may only be remotely connected to you. It's all because you are trying to prove to yourself and others that you are important. This is a big sign that your identity is lost in ministry. Because when you are there to serve, you will be giving others credit for their part, not just trying to find opportunities to validate yourself. When your identity isn't lost in ministry, you will be a better team player who desires celebrating wins together instead of pointing out your individual performance.

- **You no longer have any friends**
You can end up with very few personal friends outside of ministry, when your identity becomes lost in ministry. This can happen because you don't think you can relate to non-ministry people. It can also happen because you say you are too busy. I've heard this one a few times with other leaders:

> *"I just don't have time to hang out anymore. I'm trying to lead 2,000 people!"*

> *"I've got 2,000 people wanting to spend time with me. I'm sure my old friends understand"*

Healthy leaders like King David recognise the influence of a brotherly friendship.

David would never have sacrificed the friendship with Jonathan, had he been given a choice. And even after Jonathan's death, he honoured him. They loved each other. The people of the Bible had a much higher regard and commitment to friendship than we do these days. We are often too quick to forfeit friendships in place of careers, calling, our marriages, our children. We are often forfeiting a lot for the roles we play in church. The Bible never suggests that friendship is secondary to everything else. Jonathan and David arguably made each other better, as the verse suggests: *"As iron sharpens iron, so one person sharpens another"* (Proverbs 27:17). This verse is not clear in who the *'another'* could be. It could be a spouse, it could be a parent, a brother, your neighbour or a friend. In spite of what the world has tried to tell us, marriage doesn't meet every social or companionship need. If you want a better marriage, have friends and not just your 'couple' friends so you can hang out together. If you want a better ministry experience, have and keep your friends. It is incredibly short sighted to let go of friendships for the sake of ministry. Unfortunately, people in your church don't appreciate you as much as you think. They may seem desperate to hang out with you now, but once you aren't there, they don't reach out nearly as much as you were. But to make decisions to let go of friendships for ministry, will eventually isolate you. We need friends, even if it's just for the sake of not being alone at the end of it all.

☐ **You work when you're not supposed to be**
There are times when you will have to do extra work. It's the project nature of church. There are always events and programs happening. But, if in your quiet times at home, you find yourself picking up the computer and doing work? And maybe those are times when you could be participating in your hobbies, or spending time with family? Maybe it has

become too important to you.

In a rather large nutshell, your identity loss to ministry looks like **obsession**. True obsession is another form of enslavement. It's possessive and tormenting. You can't rest, you can't wake, without serving the obsession. The biblical terminology would be **idolatry**. Nobody said that idolatry was always about objects. Idolatry can be relating to a concept. Idolatry and the worship of an idol isn't always about adoration either. It can also be about fixation. It is whatever consumes your life, to the point of dependency. Just like the verse says, "*For where your treasure is, your heart will be also*" (Matthew 6:21). God is the only one you can 'consume', that fills, refreshes and strengthens. Any idolatry, including ministry, simultaneously consumes you, as you consume it. Which means you are never full, and always hungry.

I had to repent when I finished up in ministry. I can tell you with absolute confidence that every point I have listed above, I personally experienced at some point in ministry. I feel ashamed to admit that, but I am happy to embarrass myself for the sake of future leaders. I started out as just being excited to serve God, and somehow I ended up being engrossed by ambition. Every sign that might have given me an indication of my value as a pastor, was scrutinised. Toward the end, I was a wreck. Obsession is exhausting. I took three months off at the beginning of 2019 as recovery time post-ministry before really progressing with this book. For the first week of rest, I would sit in my chair and simply lament over how lost I felt without ministry. Shortly thereafter, the Holy Spirit illuminated to me what was really going on…It was like I had finally stopped to realise just how hungry and thirsty my soul was. I had been feeding my soul lollies for years, in the form of ministry-performance. My soul was severely malnourished. But as I cried out to God to fill my hunger and my thirst, I was reminded of Psalm 34:8 *"Taste and see that the Lord is good"*. His goodness restored me. Maybe you are reading this, assuming that this can't happen to you and that I was just a really broken person. If you are telling yourself it's impossible, just be careful. Pastors have committed stranger mistakes than this. No one is beyond identity loss. Not after demonstrating earlier how unstable our identities really are. But don't listen to me, listen to the symptoms. Are they there? Identity loss will evidence itself.

Imagine what it must look like to God, when we worship and idolise ministry? It's like worshipping the walls of the temple, instead of what is inside. It's like being in awe of the chocolate wrapper, instead of the chocolate. Actually, it's worse than that. It's like eating the chocolate wrapper, instead of the chocolate. Ministry is the vehicle for leading others to intimacy with Christ. We do it, so that they will eat the chocolate. If we know that the chocolate is so good, why are we standing there eating the wrapper? Yeah I know, we never intend to eat the wrapper. But when the wrapper is the one bit we can influence, we get distracted. We forget that without the incredible life-defining chocolate, there is no need for a wrapper.

Identity gain

Guys probably don't understand this so much, but for women if we are having a down day it can do wonders to dress yourself up a bit. There's something about it that activates confidence and good feelings. You can try to tell yourself for hours, how valuable you are, and it have no effect. But the moment you wear a nice outfit, do your hair, and put on some makeup…you feel valuable. No need to thank me lads, I've probably given you a lot of understanding now as to why it takes so long for ladies to get ready. By the way, I know some lads who could challenge a woman with the time it takes to get ready…so take it easy on the agreement.

There are a few great passages in scripture that talk about the concept of 'putting on':

- Isaiah 61:3 *Put on a garment of praise*
- Romans 13:14 *Clothe yourselves with the Lord Jesus Christ*
- Galatians 3:27 *For all of you who were baptised into Christ have clothed yourselves with Christ*
- Colossians 3:12 *Therefore, as God's chosen people, holy and dearly loved, clothe yourselves with compassion, kindness, humility, gentleness and patience.*
- 1 Peter 5:5 *Clothe yourselves with humility*

It's interesting to me how, in society, we often wear clothes according to our identity and status. Business men wear business suits. Rich people wear expensive clothing. Our clothes have been used for centuries to communicate to ourselves and others the status we hold in society. Kings and queens wear crowns. Priests wear robes. Hipsters have beards. Rockers wear flannel. We wear clothes to reflect who we believe we are. Maybe you don't think about clothes that much. But I would hazard a guess that you wouldn't wear something that presents you as polar opposite to who you think you are. That is, you aren't going to wear punk clothes, if you don't like punk music. In classic counter-cultural 'fashion', God reverses the order. Instead of our clothes being a reflection of who we are, we put the clothes on to BECOME who we now are in Christ. What beautiful symbolism. How significant is it that Jesus in John 11:44 instructs Lazarus whom He has raised from the dead to *"Take off the grave clothes"*

There are a few actions you can take to restore your identity, but the first one is to *'take off the grave clothes'* and *'put on'* the new garments Christ has given you. Do it again if you have to. Put on His righteousness. This is who you are. The redeemed. You might be a pastor and you might be a leader. But that is secondary to you being a child of God. Repent and change your clothes.

The clothes we have been given in Christ are way more significant than the ones you wear in life. Put on the new identity you've been given.

Give me some practicals, Mel!

Yes, I love the theoretical and the imagery of the clothes, but I know you need some rock-solid ideas of what you can do. Many years ago, I read this marvellous book about developing habits. It's called "*Making Habits Breaking Habits*"[17] by Jeremy Dean. There are so many takeaways from that book. If you want to change an existing habit, research suggests you need to replace it. I suppose this might be the theory behind those fake cigarettes. My point is, that when you have had your identity submerged in ministry, you

> **God is understanding, and offers true validation**

inevitably have developed psychological and behavioural patterns that if not addressed continue to reinforce the ministry-identity you've adopted. When I was feeling particularly vulnerable to exclusion, I noticed a depressive mood would overshadow me each Thursday. I guess after several days of feeling isolated at my desk, I started to feel pretty unimportant. Which wouldn't have bothered me of course, if I weren't looking for validation. Every week, the message kept on being reinforced. "You're not important. They don't care about you." So, I needed to do something to break the psychological habit I had created. I sat down and worked out when it was happening and the specific circumstances. I isolated the feeling to a time and day, and I strategised my way out of it. When Thursday came around, I would pick up a laptop and work outside in the coffee shop. Being around other people, helped me not feel so isolated.

All of the suggestions that follow are intended to replace the bad habits that have caused you to lose identity and to restore your real identity:

- **Don't sit in the front row, take the smaller office, decline a meeting or two**

    Luke 11:43 says "*Woe to you Pharisees, because you love the most important seats in the synagogues...*" Jesus said that, so don't point the finger at me if you think it's harsh. When you are seeking validation, you desire to be in important places. If you can afford to not attend a meeting talk to your Senior Pastor about it and refrain from attending, if that suits them. The principle here is to starve the desire. It's kind of like an addiction really. If you want to stop a habit, you have to stop

IDENTITY LOSS

feeding it...until it dies. Even better, find something to replace it with. Instead of sitting on the front row, go and help the team at the back. Instead of taking the big office, take the small one. Instead of attending the meeting that your Senior Pastor has cleared you to miss, get out of the office and visit someone who really needs company. Instead of going on those 'lunch dates' that the Senior Pastor does every now and then, go spend an hour in your community department packing food parcels. Not always, just infrequently. Behave like those things aren't important to you, and it will force your heart and mind to catch up. Just a warning, initially this will be painful or even elicit anger from within yourself. Because you are going actively against what your validation-hungry heart desires. Deal with those thoughts with God. Prayerfully and honestly bring them to Him. Ask for His strength to endure, so that you can be healed.

- **Serve when no-one is watching, do the jobs that don't improve your status**
There's nothing to test your need for validation more, than your deeds and words being invisible. Don't pray, in a prayer meeting sometimes. Or make your prayers succinct and unimpressive. Serve in a way that you know can only be for God. Do the tasks that elicit nil status points. Fill the communion cups. Clean up a mess that someone else made. Yeah, I know they don't deserve it, but do it anyway. It's for your benefit, not theirs. Keep your heart focused on anonymity rather than notoriety. Starve the need to impress. And when your self-validation is being rattled by your new choices, turn

to God for Him to fill that need. He's faithful. He won't leave you stranded when you are so desperate to heal. Especially since He stands to gain also from your commitment.

- **Make some friends**
  Two things about this one. Make friends with people that you aren't shepherding. The dynamic in shepherding relationships is one where you are meeting needs, and not necessarily having your needs met. These aren't always the most beneficial friendships for you. My tip, if your friends are predominantly staff members, make an effort to have friends outside of your workplace. The common ground you have with staff is church and ministry. Which is exactly what you are trying to avoid - more conversations about ministry. Also, if you are going to make friends outside of church, who might not be Christians…be careful not to only associate with them for conversion purposes. Real love is unconditional regardless of outcome. If the situation arises to share the gospel, sure go for it. But if you are only hanging out with them to bring them to Christ, it's still 'ministry'.

- **Elevate and recommend others**
  When there is an opportunity for someone, whether it's preaching, a new role, an office vacancy, a conference, leading a prayer meeting…instead of taking it, suggest someone else. Look for others growth and development. It's not wrong to take presenting opportunities, but it can be unhealthy if you already have a need to be validated and your identity is lost in ministry. There are definitely times that you should take it, so it

does require some discernment. I'm just saying that not every opportunity must be taken. This is exercised frequently in scripture. King David, Daniel, Jesus...opportunities presented themselves, but they were selective with the ones they took. This is a scary one, I know. I often would be so fearful that I would never get the opportunity again. But this is where you rely on God's promotion and timing. He will never forget it when you've put someone else before yourself. He will not disadvantage you for such choices. Also, elevate others. The number of leaders who talk about themselves, is a little annoying frankly. Be different. See the good that others do, and make a point to encourage and praise them. Privately, and in front of others. Validation makes you incredibly self-focused. So be intentional to reverse that. Be other-focused.

- **Make a plan for how you are going to respond when someone leaves**

    Even though it may hurt, make a plan for how you are going to respond. To the person, and internally. I had people quit becoming Connect Group Leaders all the time. It's not one of the easiest ministries to serve in. My programmed response was so:
    - **To the individual**

      "I'm really sorry to hear that. Is everything ok? Can our Pastoral Care team help you? You will be missed of course. Thank you so much for everything you have done for your people. I know I wouldn't even know the half of it, but I know God honours you."

- If they are actually leaving the church, and are a bit disgruntled,

    "I'm really sorry to hear that. Do you know what church you are going to go to? Can I help you find a church? I could give you a few names of some really good churches close to you. You will be missed, and we appreciate the ways in which you served your people. I know God has great plans for you."

- **Privately**

    "God, I am disappointed that __left, but I know that you are building your church. I trust that you will provide a solution for the gap, and I commit this ministry to you again. It's your ministry, not mine. And I pray that your will be done."

    And that's it. I don't beg them to stay. I don't try to change their mind. I honour their decision and I support them. I don't take it personally, I don't get defensive. And I take it to God. If my identity is not linked to my ministry, then I don't need to take it to heart when they leave.

- **Take holidays**

    Make sure you schedule in holidays. Not when you are about to fall apart. Have something to look forward to. When you are at home, spend time planning it. Allow yourself to get excited. Try to go somewhere new, so that you can think about all the exciting new adventures.

IDENTITY LOSS

- **Explore hobbies that you get lost in, read novels, watch the news, research subjects that interest you**

   When I was a teenager, I spent a lot of time playing guitar and singing in my room. I would find that the whole day would disappear, and I wouldn't even realise it. If you can find a hobby like that, you've found something good. To a degree, this book has been that for me. I have definitely lost track of time frequently in the process.

   Read stuff that has nothing to do with ministry. Books or podcasts that provoke your mind, or create that sense of wonder. Listening to Ted Talks can be a bit like that for me. I feel like my brain gets massaged a bit.

   Watch the news. I am a little ashamed to say it, but whilst I was working at the church I almost never watched or heard the news. Why is that such a big deal? Well, I had no idea what was going on in the outside world, unless someone I knew put it on Facebook. I have a massive gap in my societal understanding of about five years.

   Research interesting subjects. The strangest of all post-ministry happenings, has got to be the insane level of YouTube research I did on curly hair maintenance. I have curly hair, and I just didn't really care about maintaining it when I was working at the church. For some strange reason, when I left I went into overdrive learning about it. I enjoyed it. It wasn't because I was trying to fix a problem that was mismanaged. I just found it interesting. And my hair is thanking me for it.

- **Volunteer in the community and don't make it a church program**
  Fill a need in the community. There are so many causes outside of your church walls that you can get involved in. Do it without strings. Service doesn't have to be confined to church walls. You can extend the Kingdom without a church program. Get your hands dirty and mingle with people 'out there'. It will remind you of what it's all really about. One of my close friends was working at church, running the dance ministry. She started going out to a school that we had relationship with and teaching dance there. There were a few times that she would return and just be in tears, when she realised how significant it was to some of the kids to be given an opportunity to express themselves through dance. It was delightful to watch her heart be moved all over again for her ministry, the people and ultimately God.

  And don't turn it into a church program. Okay, sometimes you should. Especially if you are onto a cracker community-based program. My point is that if your 'ministry' benefits from the volunteering…well…it's just not really the reason you set out to volunteer. If it benefits your ministry, then it may still be validation.

- **Close your mouth**
  So, this one's really simple. Keep your mouth shut. If there is an opportunity to boast, or to big-note, take credit, or be impressive…just don't. Don't give yourself a chance to be validated that way, and allow your identity to further solidify its home in ministry. We could practise holding our tongues a bit

more anyway. I find that my self-control over my mouth tends to lack when I'm talking too much. Oh, wait a minute! That's biblical "*Too much talk leads to sin. Be sensible and keep your mouth shut*" Proverbs 10:19, NLT...I love the directness of this version. I know this can be really hard for some. I'm not suggesting you don't talk at all, I'm suggesting that you let opportunities to talk about your successes be short conversations. When you're needing validation, you will showcase your accolades. Don't give yourself a chance to reward your displaced validation. As you keep silencing that part of you, you will get stronger in it. Just like a muscle.

- **Do a study on your 'Identity in Christ'**
There are studies out there, go get one and do it by yourself if you have to. But attack this issue of identity head on. Pray about it. Ask God to show you the root of the matter. Go get counselling if it's really bad. Just take it on like an adversary. Resist the temptation to stay as you are.

Sacrifice the dream

It's possible that part of the reason your identity has become lost in ministry, is because of the specific promises God has given you. Maybe God has shown you that certain blessings are going to happen. Out of a desire to see them come to pass, we can sometimes become preoccupied with the promise. The story of Abraham and Isaac and God's' instruction to Abraham to take Isaac up the hill to be sacrificed, is probably the most un-relatable bible stories for our time. But I find myself reflecting on this story often. I find myself considering the fact that the only way you can really tell whether you love the promises of God more than God Himself, is whether you are willing to sacrifice the promise. Unfortunately, I know tonnes of people and I came pretty close myself, who wanted the promises of God more than God. And when push came to shove, they laid their relationship with God down on the altar to be sacrificed, and impatiently walked away with a counterfeit promise. Idolising ministry can do this. Just like the Israelites, the promised land rich with milk and honey, became the dream. Instead of the God who provides it. We must ask ourselves frequently am I willing to sacrifice this? If God asked me, would I let it go? Abraham obeyed not knowing that there would be another way. Will you obey Him regardless of how far away it takes you?

The Jesus factor

Did Jesus' identity get lost in ministry? It's kind of hard to say. There's no doubt he would have been tempted. He was after all the Messiah. But Jesus wasn't invested in ministry, as much as He was interested in doing His Father's will. That was the whole motivator for everything He did. He definitely wasn't seeking validation from man, and He certainly wasn't seeking the powerful Messianic welcome that the Jews wanted to give to their saviour. He knew exactly who He was, and He didn't succumb to pressure to be the Messiah everyone seemed to have planned.

If Jesus needed validation, His responses to the Pharisees' questioning would have been very different. He would have wanted to defend himself or explain his behaviour especially at the end with the threat of physical harm overshadowing His arrest. He wouldn't at all have given them the often abrupt and forward responses, because he would have cared what they were thinking. But He didn't fall into any of that. He was very clear to whom He belonged.

CHAPTER 6

Beware the bubble

If you really want to prevent identity loss, your best strategy is to 'Beware the Bubble'. There's a Simpsons episode where Bart contracts the panda virus and is required to live in a bubble for a little while. The doctors keep telling him that he will continue to live a normal life. Of course, the experience is very abnormal. Imagine attending school in a bubble?

So, what's the bubble in ministry? Ask your spouse. If you have one of course. And if you don't have a spouse, the bubble might be the reason you don't. I've heard many a spouse lament, including my own. "You guys are in a bubble". Yep, church leadership can be a big ol' bubble. What do I mean by this? You are disconnected from reality and have lost perspective about life and the real world. So here are the three main often collaborating hallmarks of the bubble:

- o **Isolation**
  To cause a person or place to remain alone or apart from others.

- o **Conformity**
  Compliance with socially accepted conventions.

- **Separation**
  To become detached or disconnected, in this case, from the outside world.

I've heard very few stories of organisations, particularly religious ones, that have maintained wholesome values and behaviours when separated from the 'world'. In the stories I've read and been told, the behaviour is significantly worsened. In an atmosphere of isolation and low accountability, delusions can be entertained, and people can be worshipped. There is a surprising number of cults in Australia and many people are involved in them. It's difficult to get exact numbers, but despite our modern educated era, people keep joining cults. Separation, isolation and conformity are apparently effective.

> Allowing yourself to be **moved**, is one of the greatest exercises in **vulnerability**

The fact is, that churches can show hallmarks of isolation, conformity and separation. Let me demonstrate how:

- What is it called when you don't have any time, nor do you make time to hang out with pre-ministry friends and family?

ISOLATION/SEPARATION

- What is it called when you have to adjust your pre-existing life conditions so significantly in order to participate in a community and lifestyle?

CONFORMITY

BEWARE THE BUBBLE

☐ What is it called when you are encouraged to participate in certain behaviours that will be rewarded in opportunity and praise like workaholism?

CONFORMITY

☐ What is it called when you are encouraged to forego whether directly or indirectly personal activities for the sake of the kingdom regardless of the reason you are encouraged to forego it?

ISOLATION

☐ What is it called when you work with and socialise with the same people every day?

ISOLATION

☐ What is it called when your whole world is made up of Christians, and you are encouraged not to expose yourself to perceived negative influences?

SEPARATION

☐ What is it called when you encourage people to come to you, instead of going out to them?

SEPARATION

Isolation, conformity and separation are the negative connotation of ideas that can otherwise be considered reasonable. All communities have the ability to influence people to conform, and sometimes the outcome is positive. It's sometimes good to isolate yourself and get away with God. It's not a bad thing to separate from your non-believing friends if they are encouraging you to sin.

Yes, you are right. There is a middle ground. I'm simply stating that isolation, conformity and separation and their degree of danger is like a continuum. Isolation in its extreme form is confinement. Conformity in its extreme is control. Separation can easily become segregation or prejudice. It's important to recognise that these are usually choices you are individually making, but the environment can provide the right climate for cultivation.

These are some factors that can happen organisationally, when a church bubble exists:

- **Overemphasise the spiritual**
  I remember once being told that I had a 'spirit of rejection'. Actually, I just don't like being rejected, like everyone else. Rejection activates the same part of the brain associated with pain. Does that mean I had a spirit? Probably not. Maybe. It's possible it just hurts when I get rejected. That's an example of over-spiritualising. Unfortunately, over spiritualisation, leaves people in a position where it's difficult to debate, because the speaker has pulled the God-card.

Christianese

You've no doubt heard of this. There are some funny videos on YouTube demonstrating the significance of the problem. Christianese language makes us so unrelatable, and it isolates non-Christians from entering our world. Why do we want people to come to faith, if they can't feel the sense of belonging they have craved their whole life? When we exclude them with our Christianese language, our complicated prayers, our processes and structures that are clearly made for the comfort of Christians, we may as well not invite them in the first place. I've heard of gang members returning to gangs after giving church a try. Because they just felt more acceptance and belonging there. That stuff breaks my heart, having come from circumstances where I didn't feel like I belonged. In my Christian journey, I can see a direct correlation between the times I have belonged and the times I grew in my faith. It had little to do with preaching, worship or events. It's always related to these basic questions that every person subconsciously asks of every community, whether Christian or not:

- Do I feel wanted? Being a welcoming church is not enough to help people feel at home.
- Am I included?
- Can I relate to people? Do I identify with them?
- Can I be myself fully without fear of rejection or judgement?
- Do I feel a part of this?

Imbalanced view of the world

The world is hurting. But not everyone, all the time. Christians aren't always having fun. Sometimes they are hurting. When you are in the bubble, your perspective gets warped about stuff like that. When the Queensland Abortion Bill was up for consideration, it felt like it was what everyone was talking about. I saw articles on Facebook and Instagram posts. It was a discussion in Connect Groups. And rightly so! It is a worthy discussion for Christians to engage in. Anyhow, I was over at my mum's house one day and I asked her what she thought about the Abortion Bill. She said, "What about it?" She didn't really know much about it. My mum watches the news, she reads the newspaper. She's aware of current issues in our society. In fact, she is probably more aware of what is going on than myself. But she really didn't comprehend the whole issue. Is it possible that the bulk of our debates were being heard by people who are already convinced? Was anyone hearing us in the outside world? Of course, I know there are faithful Christians out there consistently interjecting in such debates. But maybe our biggest agendas, are not really the same as the world's. Obvious, I know. But shouldn't that change our approach?

Us and them

If there is one thing that the Royal Commission into religious institutional responses to child sex abuse demonstrated, is that we can no longer point our finger and say, 'the problem is out there!' Evidently, the church has had a massive problem with sin and secrecy. It's actually the same with the homosexual debate. There are more people in our congregations than we probably realise struggling with their sexuality or who ticked 'yes' to gay marriage in Australia. The lines between the world and the church are a lot more blurred than they used to be. Well I presume the lines were clearer in the past. Maybe it wasn't, and people were just silent. Whilst we are pointing our fingers outward, saying 'they, they, they'...we are blind to the reality of the struggles within our own ranks.

- **Everything becomes about the bubble**
  When you are in the bubble, you think everything revolves around the bubble. This is a symptom of disconnection from the outside world. You think everything is about your specific church, or your denomination to the point where you don't acknowledge other organisations and churches that are doing the same Kingdom activities. Sometimes other churches are even seen as competitors instead of partners in God's Kingdom. You can start to believe that everything is about building your church, instead of recognising that God also wants to bring His Kingdom values to your community.

This is what may happen to individuals caught in the bubble:

- **Few real friends**
  I define real friends as a person you can tell your biggest, darkest secrets and your greatest fears. Do you have friends like that, besides your spouse? You need friends like that in ministry. If you don't have that, get a counsellor or a coach. Have someone you can be real enough with, because healing is experienced through confession. James 5:16..."

- **Isolates your family**

    You may not realise it, but your family can feel pretty isolated. To a degree this may be less so with the spouse of a Senior Pastor…but largely your family are unknown. They are often introduced as Pastor's wife, husband or child. So, their identity in your congregation revolves around you. They have to be careful who they speak to because of your calling. They are often expected to adopt the same character and expectations you are expected to have. They may be judged by the same standard as you. They feel alone when you are attending meetings throughout the week. And on Sundays when you are busy, they have to sit by themselves. I don't know what the solution is to this problem. But they suffer for the bubble. Which means either you have to try and get out of it as much as you can, or they have no choice but to come into it, which is not necessarily a great solution.

- **Judgmentalism**

    Judgmentalism is one-part pride, one-part separation. When you are out in the world listening to people's challenges, there is no way you can judge them so harshly. I met someone recently who has the worst abuse story I have ever heard. For some reason, I get a lot of people confiding in me about their abuse stories. So, I've heard a lot. And this one was by far the worst. So, when they told me that they had been a part of a gang and did things that they now feel ashamed about, I didn't judge him. My heart was full of compassion. How could I even begin to understand the damage caused to their heart and mind by the abuse they endured? And everybody has their own story.

Without God, what hope do people have? Even with God, it's hard to live a faithful life. I'd say it's the reason Paul talked so often about standing firm. Because just staying strong, is hard enough. One of the most marvellous qualities of Jesus, is His compassion. He was frequently moved. It's in His nature. Compassion is one of the traits of the Saviour, that I try very hard to emulate. My husband and I have even talked about how to cultivate this quality in our daughter because we see it as a critical quality of a true disciple. Compassion is one of the most powerful emotions. Compassion can make you change direction. Compassion can make you give up everything. Allowing yourself to be moved, is one of the greatest exercises in vulnerability. Like Mother Teresa, who lived with the poor in the slums, compassion moved her to complete abandonment of any personal desires. There is no room for judgement, when compassion fills your heart. I'm not talking about pity. I'm talking about compassion. Get close enough to get your hands dirty. Allow yourself to be moved, and I would bet that there would be very little room for judgement.

Skewed priorities

When you are in the bubble, you can lose perspective about what is really important in life. The lost are important. Helping the poor is important. Helping widows and those needing an advocate are important. Your family is important. Whether you have the right attire to fit in at the next conference? Not critical. Whether enough people put their hands up during worship? Feels important, but actually it's not that important. If you have the right coffee table in your office? Not that important. Nice, but not critical. There are a whole bunch of things that we can start to care about when our only society is Christians. They will openly criticise, judge, and hurt. And they justify their unloving actions all because they think the Bible suggests that the carpet should be a certain colour. Before you know, we are all working really hard to accommodate these Christians who probably just need to grow up. When you are in the bubble, you think you need to appease those people because the absolute worst-case scenario is them leaving. Whilst I have grace and mercy for people, sometimes I think you should just let them leave. Hear me out…If you have to change your strategy and activities, because people are going to complain…just do the strategy. Now I don't think you should be haphazard about that. If people have complaints, listen to them just in case you are totally wrong. Validate their needs, work with them as much as possible…but don't change the conviction you have in your heart about God's plan for your people. Let them go. Numbers aren't that important. Don't lose perspective. Them leaving is not the worst thing that could happen. They'll go somewhere else. Their faith is not going to fall apart and if it does that is on them. Not following through with a God-idea that could lead to transformation in your community…that is the worst thing that could happen. PLEASE NOTE: this is not a licence to be arrogant and inconsiderate. If you have been rude and hurtful, and they leave and their faith falls apart, that's not cool. No strategy will justify poor behaviour toward the brethren.

☐ You are motivated to help people because you want to change them, not love them

When you are disconnected from non-believers your motivation can become about changing them. Because they need a saviour right? Yes, the world is in need of a saviour. But so are Christians. We never stop needing Him. When you hang out with non-believers, and you try to 'fix' them you might discover a few things:

- o They don't think they need to be changed and all you get is resistance to any God conversations. You also send a message that Jesus' agenda is to change them because He thinks they aren't good enough, instead of to save them.
- o They start to distrust you, because it's clear to them that you have an agenda. Worst case scenario, they think you're only hanging out with them to 'convert' them.
- o They don't appreciate being looked down upon. It sends a message that you are superior to them. And you're not. It's only Christ's grace and righteousness that has made you who you are. We aren't necessarily better, we are freer.

Even though, we do want to see people come to faith, our commitment, according to Christ is to love them. You might argue that the most loving act is to share the gospel. But I would argue that it's not, if you're being forceful about it. Love is patient, love is kind. It's not forceful. If you are being pushy about it, you might not really be thinking about them. Pushy-ness doesn't really look that different from a used car salesman, who evidently is never really thinking about the buyer when he's trying to offload that old Commodore.

- **Organisational goals outweigh individual goals**
This is an interesting tension. If there is someone wanting to be promoted, but there isn't really anywhere for them to go and there is no budget for it…you bet that the organisational goals will outweigh the individual ones. If you are being asked to be out five nights a week, and you haven't been able to play basketball for six weeks? Or you've missed date night for a while? Not cool. We all do hours outside of work, but it's unreasonable for you have to give up everything. You are allowed to be a human being, and have outside interests. Especially if it makes you a better leader. And it does. Being a balanced human being is of great value to your leadership. If someone has to work on a Sunday, and can't volunteer in your area anymore? Give them a break! They need money. Are you going to give them money? Are you going to pay for their meals? Of course not. The goals of the organisation shouldn't completely outweigh the individual's goals. When you are in a bubble, your world is the church and you can come to expect it to be the same for everyone else. You can come to forget how hard it is to do a full-time job, and volunteer. Should we not have standards? Of course, we should. But just ensure that your standards are achievable for someone

> Jesus couldn't be **possessed** by any one **group**

who has other components to their life, and not just achievable for you and your ministry-obsessed self.

We were never meant to live in a bubble. It's fear and comfort that influences our desire to live in one. On the other hand, Jesus speaks frequently about how we are supposed to be represented in the world.

Matthew 5:16 says:

> *"In the same way, let your light shine before others..."*

Being in a bubble makes it really hard to be anything to anyone beyond the bubble. Let alone a shining light. That's why it's called a bubble…

What do you do about it?

The best thing to do, is resist every urge that could draw you into the bubble. It's essentially the same list featured in the previous chapter. The action plan is the same. Maintain a personal life. Have interests and hobbies. Have goals that don't have anything to do with ministry. Learn a language. Be a human, and protect all efforts in that pursuit.

The Jesus factor

If Jesus was ever tempted by a 'bubble'-like lifestyle, it would have been by associating Himself with the Pharisees. Jesus did have a few situations where he mingled positively with Pharisees. On several occasions He dined with Pharisees (Luke 7:36, Luke 11:37 and Luke 14:1). In John 3, Nicodemus, a Pharisee, comes to Jesus and affirms that He has come from God. If Jesus cared about the Pharisees, He could have been caught up in their world.

He would have been rewarded too, with power, status and wealth. But the Pharisees' bubble was not at all what He came to be a part of. He says it Himself...He came for the sick. He came to seek and save the lost. Jesus may have had the disciples, but He lived His life well and truly outside of the bubble of the religious world of that day. He roamed. He couldn't be possessed by any one group. We ought to be careful to become too comfortable in groups that will prevent us from meeting those who Jesus came for.

CHAPTER 7

You will get discouraged

Recently we celebrated our daughter's' sixth birthday. We couldn't do a massive party, so we negotiated: a small gathering of four friends, a cake and a few simple decorations. Oh, and of course cupcakes for school. It was really nice, and I could tell she felt blessed. In classic Mel and Josh fashion though, we basically still had some of the decorations around the house for almost a month after. One Christmas we didn't pack down the Christmas tree until about April! I know, we are slackers. Anyhow, one of our dogs was in the house a few days after the party and I guess he just presumed that one of the balloons was a ball. He loves chasing a ball, so I threw the balloon in the air a few times for him. He was enjoying himself until he grabbed the balloon with his teeth, and it popped. Right in his face! Not a big surprise to me of course, but his face was about as deflated as that balloon. Poor fella.

Deflated, is how I would describe discouragement. Apologies, that this wasn't a smoother segue or that it led to a lousy topic. Discouragement is intense. It can come on suddenly, or slowly. Either way, it's really hard to shift. Even though you can talk positively to yourself and speak the Word of God, it can be pretty persistent. Like a dark cloud that lurks in the recesses of your heart, reducing the effect of the light. Every leader goes through discouragement at some time, if they are in it for long enough. And often it's one of the hardest battles to win.

Where did you come from?

After such a crummy year, I figured I'd take three weeks off to recuperate and just forget that my church existed for a bit. The process for the change in leadership had come to an end, which naturally required readjustments. We were now entering the interim phase. But we didn't know for how long we would be in this interim phase. We were in the worse kind of holding pattern: one without a timeline and no way of estimating one. The three weeks off were good and timely. I relaxed, went swimming, spent time with family. But another really cool thing happened that I didn't anticipate. I had some time for self-discovery. One of the elders had been really encouraging me and gave me a few chances to try new opportunities. He let me MC a service. He let me contribute to some strategy type meetings. He even started talking about an opportunity to take on a role of sorts that would allow me to contribute to bigger discussions like discipleship. It felt really good to know that someone believed in me again. Especially since my self-belief was beginning to wane. So, whilst I was on holidays, I had this massive revelation that started off in a kind of peculiar place. I realised that I wasn't the leader I used to be. When I worked in the secular workplace, I was so different. I was courageous. Nothing really got me

> Peace and joy are fruits of the **Spirit**. They are largely an **internal** experience.

down. Every time a change would happen that would take me back a few steps, I would just stop, make a plan and execute the plan. I was a very focused and enthusiastic leader. A go-getter! And I was rewarded with a decent income, influence and trust. I got chances to study with my expenses paid, and I got to speak at significant forums and places that other people weren't. And best of all, I got to innovate, and my colleagues trusted me to lead them into new adventures. During my holidays, I realised that something had changed in me since working in a church. I wasn't the same leader. In fact, I almost felt like I had forgotten who I was. And that entrepreneurial, innovative spirit that I had, was such a distant memory it made me wonder if I was observing someone else's life.

   I got this sense, that the Holy Spirit was reminding me to give me courage again. That I could lead through this new season and be an influencer. I could help participate in the new future of our church. By the end of the three weeks, there was an excitement bubbling up in me. I knew the terrain was going to be hard, but we had a chance to start afresh...and I was going to do my best to be a part of the solution. However, in less than three months that positivity was on its deathbed. A lot happened, that escalated into much larger problems. Whilst some confidence had restored in me, it was evident that others weren't prepared for my renewal. I had dreams about being pursued by polar bears, and I felt much the same in my waking hours. That discouragement became depression which unfolded into 10 months of turbulence. I didn't think that it could be more painful than the previous year...I was so incredibly wrong.

What is it? What does it look like?

For the most part we all know what discouragement is. In general, it's a loss of confidence, and a loss of hope. It's being disheartened. From a spiritual perspective, it's also experienced as a loss of faith. There are degrees of discouragement. Sometimes it's an 'oh, that wasn't great', but the situation doesn't devastate your life. And there are some discouragements that are like being punched in the guts or not being able to breathe. It often depends on how significant the situation is, to the individual. I haven't personally been on the receiving end of significant racism, only a few inappropriate comments here and there. But I've been told that the first time you are on the receiving end of a really racist experience, it's like being physically punched in the guts. In fact, I've heard that description for other prejudices too. The punch-in-the-guts moment usually combines with a lot of other emotions. Like shock, rejection, anger, and confusion. People can feel physically ill from such an experience. Shock alone can make you literally physically ill. It's like you've finally woken up to something, even if it's just that you are different, and that people make a distinction when they look at you. The thought that something about you, that you have no control over, is a limitation on your experience of life, is a very hard concept to reconcile. Some people never get over that experience. It's trauma.

So how can you tell if you or someone else is discouraged? Here's the signs and symptoms:

- **You doubt your call**
  Discouragement certainly makes you wonder if you are

supposed to be doing ministry. Discouragement makes you wonder if you are good for anything. There are a lot of challenges in ministry, and not always a lot of direct reward. But doubting your call, isn't really about the unfavourable circumstances that you often find yourself in. It's more personal. It's wondering if you are the right person. It's wondering if you really can do this for an extended period of time. It's assuming that there is some innate inadequacy that disqualifies you from ever really seeing the fruit that you think you ought to have.

At some point, you've looked at yourself and the requirements for ministry and noticed a gap. The gap is the cause of your confusion. God got it wrong, right? Why would He choose someone who doesn't quite make the cut? It may even start with, "Why me? Why would you choose me?" And the tone during that questioning, is not one of self-loathing. It's a tone of genuine bewilderment. My own times of doubt were usually focused on my role as a young mum in ministry. It would be "Why would you chose a young mum?" Let's be honest, ministry isn't always designed for families. You can't always meet congregation members during the week, when you have your work hours. You're often working around them, which means nights. I just couldn't understand why God had chosen someone who had such obvious limitations on their capacity. But God chooses who He chooses. We don't necessarily know why.

☐ **You don't feel excited anymore**
People often describe a sensation of numbness in ministry.

Even the good doesn't feel that great. If someone has a breakthrough, you are happy for them, but it doesn't invigorate your passion. Most days you struggle to get up in the morning, and coming to work seems like such a hassle. Your motivation and focus can wane significantly when you are discouraged. The underlying belief or statement is "What's the point?" In this mindset, a leader is coming to terms with this sense that nothing really changes and that any efforts to bring change aren't really worth it. So why bother? And there is actually some truth in this belief. Whether you are doing well or good, someone is always criticising you. At least that's what it looks like. Whether it's your bosses or your people. So, it seems easier to just give up on trying to manage those expectations. Of course, the reason you bother is because of God, not the people. We ultimately serve God.

You might also describe it as going through the motions. It's that feeling of monotony. Every Sunday starts to look essentially the same. Every staff meeting looks pretty well the same. The problem is that going through the motions, can become obligatory rather than fuelled by desire. Obligation doesn't produce the finest work. It produces minimal engagement. The deception of obligation is that you presume you have limited choices. You fall victim to the beast of duty. But you aren't a victim. You never are in God. So somehow you have to remind yourself you have choices, what are they, and are you willing to consider them?

- **You've become defensive and/or inactive**
If you are defensive about everything, there is a good chance that you've become so accustomed to criticism and judgement

that you see it in places that aren't really warranted. On the other hand, when you are discouraged you can also become inactive and passive, because it's taking you so much just to be present, let alone take action. The really interesting phenomenon is when you are defensive and passive. Whilst realising that you aren't really doing a lot, and your commitment is largely to surviving, you simultaneously will defend yourself passionately. Sometimes that unreasonable defensiveness is demonstrating the lack of activity. Because why would a person feel the need to defend so fervently if there isn't any truth in it? This is an occasion where you haven't got the resilience in that moment to hear something that you don't want to hear. And when you are discouraged, it doesn't take a lot to tip you over the edge so it's better to protect yourself.

- **You are jealous and envious of others**
The new bubbly staff member is the most annoying person when you are in this place of discouragement. Their positive outlook and can-do attitude is just enough to make you sick. But there is more to it than that. Deep down you kind of wish you felt like that again. You miss the days when ministry was exciting, and you didn't know all that you now know about it. You tell yourself that they'll find out soon enough, but actually you want them to find out that ministry stinks. That it doesn't deliver what it promises. That it's painful and hard. It's kind of a misdirected subtle revenge on ministry, to see them struggle. So, whilst you may feel jealous and envious emotionally, its stemming from anger toward the matter that has really disappointed you: Ministry. And potentially God.

☐ **You have the "if only…" mindset**
When we intuitively know that life doesn't feel right, we will look for answers. Inevitably, human behaviour is to look to the external circumstances or people as responsible:

> "If only they would let me…"
> "If only they didn't leave…"
> "If only she didn't…"

And on and on it goes. In my own stage of disappointment, my 'if only' was:

> "If only I wasn't doing Connect Groups anymore"

There are times when you are meant to change, and the unsettledness inside is indicative of a need to move on. But I just assumed that a position change was needed. Instead, God had a completely different plan for me.

If we believe scripture though, then we realise that peace and joy are fruits of the Spirit. They are largely an internal experience that permeates through to the external. So, assuming that an external circumstance is going to resolve the inner warring, is simply not going to work in the long run. Even if you experience momentarily changes, it won't last.

☐ **You've become cynical**
When you are sitting in a staff meeting, listening to other people get excited and your inner dialogue is saying "here we go again!" sarcastically…that's cynicism. I found myself doing

this a lot at one stage. Initially it started off as just confusion. I felt like every staff meeting it would be the same thing, "God is moving! God is doing something!" My thoughts started off saying things like, "I don't really see a difference to every other week". I had doubts that the statements were genuinely highlighting the acts of God. Especially when the measurables didn't indicate that anything was really changing. People were still leaving as quickly as new people were coming. We were still doing the same events with the same turn up, that reaped the same number of attendees. I was more annoyed that statements like that were being made subjectively, without any real evidence that it was true. Actually, looking back my initial internal debates probably weren't so bad. But, it became full blown cynicism for a period there. Because I started to filter every comment through a negative perspective. I had written off all statements I would hear in that context, instead of just the few that didn't quite make sense.

- **You don't feel like being around other people**
There is usually all the social stuff that happens after church, which develops connection and community. But when you are feeling discouraged, the last thing you want to do is hang around people. For some introverts you don't want to hang out that much anyway. But there is a different flavour to this when you are discouraged. It's an escapism.

Socialising requires energy, of which you usually have little. Even extroverts can start to recede when they are discouraged. It's not so much that the process of socialisation is exhausting, but it's the energy required to be the leader everyone wants you to be in those kinds of moments. Congregation members expect you to be caring, and always available, ready to listen. But maintaining interest in a person's cat being sick, when you are on the verge of giving up on life in general requires a lot of energy. That requires a level of energy that you just don't have when you're feeling discouraged.

- **You doubt the future can change**
When you are truly discouraged, it is incredibly hard to mobilise any kind of strength to believe that life and ministry could change. It's not that you don't want it to change, it's just that you've been stuck in the same scenario for so long it's hard to perceive that change is even possible. The Proverb makes complete sense here *"Hope deferred makes the heart sick"* Proverbs 13:12. In a place of sustained uncertainty particularly if there are other painful happenings at the same time, you can't even see a horizon anymore. Job 19:8 describes this kind of discouragement well:

> *"He has blocked my way so I cannot pass; he has shrouded my paths in darkness".*

The issue is, that our hope is supposed to be in God. Not in the circumstances. It is so hard to do, believe me. But you don't realise that your hopes and faith have been in a circumstance or person until you are let down. Somehow, at that place of disappointment, God's intention is for you to redirect your hope into Him. It's classic Israelite behaviour to put our hopes and faith in a circumstance or person. The Israelites wanted the land with milk and honey, but weren't really concerned about the provider, who could have given them that and so much more. Their hopes were in the promised land. They wanted a Messiah who would come with might and power. They had a vision of what the Messiah would be like. They weren't interested in knowing the real God and Messiah, because the Messiah they had designed was one they could put their hope in. Because ultimately their hope was for revolution and disempowering the rule over them, being restored as the chosen people. Their hopes weren't in God or the Messiah, deep down. It was in a change in circumstance.

- **You don't feel like yourself**
  You remember being happier, funnier, and more excited about life, but it seems so long ago. You wonder what happened to the person you used to be. Discouragement changes a person's demeanour. Absolutely. It's like a flattened version of yourself. This is usually a sign to me that the discouragement has been sustained for a significant enough period to affect a person's makeup and subconscious behaviour. It's a real shame that discouragement can do that, but when the rug is taken from underneath you, it has the potential to change everything. Personality is no exception.

- **You discourage others about ministry**
  When others are keen and excited about the prospect of ministry, you feel the need to come in and remind them of how hard it is. In fact, based on what you now know, you don't really think many people can do it. We aren't wrong to want to give newbies a realistic perspective of ministry. But discouraging others, is a sure sign that you've been discouraged.

  Ministry is not what is wrong, it's us. There are some issues with how ministry is done that make it particularly difficult. But we are the ones who believed it would do something for us, that it would make us feel a certain way. Often the romantic image we have of it in the beginning, is because we believe it's going to bring some sense of satisfaction or significance that we don't think other areas in life can do. That vision goes unchecked and we end up blaming ministry. The title of this book is deliberately ironic - ministry doesn't stink. Ministry is ministry. We just have really high expectations of it. It's like marriage. People get married, it doesn't work out. So, they blame marriage? Marriage: an age-old institution that has equally rewarded and troubled many in society. Marriage didn't perpetrate a crime against us. It's a human issue. We don't default to love, harmony, unity and selflessness. Especially if life isn't going well, and you aren't receiving as much as you are giving. It goes against our nature. Marriage isn't the problem. Ministry isn't the problem. So, recognise when your words and actions are discouraging others against ministry. It may not be the same for them. It certainly might, and they may have to go through all the same challenges as you. But that doesn't make ministry not worth doing.

- **You feel tired even when you've slept**
  Interestingly burnout is not always related to being driven and working long hours. It can also relate to discouragement. That's what I would define as an emotional burnout. Psychologists often term it as emotional fatigue or emotional exhaustion. Emotional exhaustion is believed to be caused by sustained stress. Just an FYI, stress isn't that heightened overwhelming

YOU WILL GET DISCOURAGED

feeling. It's just pressure. Sometimes the pressure is small, sometimes it's big and in your face. Regardless, if it is sustained it can affect your energy levels. Stress can be as a result of internal pressures too. It's not always external. So, for example, if you have a high level of anxiety and you are daily pushing back thoughts or over analysing details that you are afraid of...that is a form of stress. It exhausts you emotionally to deal with that. Feeling like you are unable to exercise power and autonomy over your life, is a stressor. When it's sustained, it can cause emotional exhaustion. So, pay attention to your energy levels, they may be trying to tell you something.

☐ **You've lost the ability to take risks**
There is a certain level of excitement and energy required to take risks. But when you're discouraged you aren't necessarily looking for a new idea to change things, or a new initiative. Because deep down you've resigned to the fact that nothing changes. Taking risks, also means that there is some kind of negative outcome that may prevail. And often your self-esteem can't handle another blow, especially not the kind of failure that can come from trying something new that collapses. That kind of failure can leave a leader quite vulnerable, because everyone can see it, question and criticise it. So often leaders, when they are discouraged, simply won't take any risks. An overarching theme of discouragement is the desire to make things 'easy'. Or what's 'easiest' or 'easier'. Even reusing old ideas/methods is a sign of discouragement, because of its underpinning desire to make things 'easy'. Tried and

tested, is easy. Tried and tested, is secure. And when you are discouraged you'd rather feel safe.

- **You are participating in self-medicating behaviours or sin**
You may not be using drugs, you might not be binge drinking alcohol, but you certainly could be overeating or over-caffeinating. You may be binge watching TV. Or maybe you are visiting places that you shouldn't be. I've heard a few occasions whereby young pastors struggle with pornography. Young people in general struggle with pornography. But even pornography can be a self-medicating behaviour. The nature of self-medication is that you've reached a point where it is easier to turn to an activity to anaesthetise your emotions, than to acknowledge them. Often it can be that a leader doesn't really know how to face them. And when silence is the prevailing theme of leadership, lest we are judged as unstable, leaders suffer with sin in silence. Sin in ministry, is not always relating to escapism. Sometimes it's also relating to pride and power. But that doesn't negate that leaders have deduced that we would rather them deal with challenges alone where sinful escapisms can flourish, than to come to us. They are concluding that we don't want to hear from them, unless it's good. Leaders presume we won't help them, if they are truly low. That they won't find compassion, rather than judgement, on the other end of their vulnerability.

- **Your heart literally feels heavy or you've got depression**
You might already have been diagnosed with depression. But if not, you might be experiencing a general heaviness of

the heart. You feel weighed down and sometimes you don't even really feel like looking up. That is a pretty strong sign of discouragement. There's a strange sensation too when you are discouraged, where you feel like your breath is laboured. Or maybe you have to sigh a lot. Apparently there is some medical basis for this. Something to do with oxygen being limited when you are sad, angry or depressed. Discouragement starts as an emotion, that may have generated from some thoughts. As it becomes persistent, behaviours emerge.

There's been a fair bit of media coverage in the Christian world about pastors who have committed suicide. It has been simply awful to read the stories. It is the saddest thing to think that there are pastors who could feel so alone and so out of options. But in reality, I know it all too well. I too came very close to giving up. Closer than I would like to have been. In the worst stages of my discouragement, I found myself sitting in my green chair flooded with thoughts of killing myself. I felt so utterly trapped and alone. The possibility was so real, that I made an agreement with myself. I told myself that as long as I sat still and didn't move, I was safe. Because I knew the moment I moved I was going to walk toward something that could end my life. I sat in that chair for three hours! For three hours the enemy persisted in telling me that suicide was the only option. For three hours I battled him, with the last bits of resilience I had in me which wasn't a lot. All my strength was being directed toward my hands that were holding me in place in that chair. But my mind was frequently falling victim to the enemy's onslaught. Thankfully it all ended when my husband returned home. I didn't even tell him the extent of what was going on. He knew I was significantly down over some events that had happened the previous day. I didn't have the energy to tell him. A few days later, I was in a counselling appointment and talked about everything. I drove home again, to an empty house and sat in my green chair. I spoke to God. If there was ever a time that I heard the voice of God clearly, it was that day. He said:

> *"How could you ever think that the world would be better off without you?"*

That was the end of any thoughts of suicide. And believe me, life got way worse after that. But the thoughts stopped.

The one thing that I haven't loved about the articles regarding these young men who committed suicide, is the fact that their pre-existing depression was significantly highlighted. Yes, they did have pre-existing conditions, but the way it was written implied that ministry doesn't have the ability to lead people to such a dark place. I have had some tough things happen in my life, but prior to 2018, I was never told by any medical practitioner that I had depression. Ministry was the most significant factor. I feel it's important to make that distinction so that we don't let ourselves off the hook for the ways in which we make ministry harder than it needs to be. And recognise that there is some corporate responsibility that needs to be taken for the vast number of leaders who have fallen behind on account of depression.

Why does it happen?

Not everyone reading this book may have yet come face to face with discouragement. So, it is still necessary to list out the various reasons it occurs:

YOU WILL GET DISCOURAGED

- **Betrayal**
Most leaders are really surprised by the fact that they may be betrayed in ministry. But unfortunately, it happens a lot. Whether it's someone talking behind your back, or divulging your secrets, or people you trust dobbing you in to some other authority. We love it when people are loyal to us. Loyalty builds faith and trust. And with trust you often give people more. More of yourself, more responsibility. That's why it hurts so much when that loyalty can turn to disloyalty. For the most part, people usually believe that they are doing the right thing when they do this. Other times, they actually want to get back at you for something. Either way, it really hurts.

- **Misunderstanding**
This is bound to happen in life and generally speaking, if you can rectify misunderstandings it can often build better relationships. On the other hand, sometimes people don't want to know what you really meant. The worst part about being misunderstood, is that you are often continued to be punished for something that may not have been correct. Also, if you aren't given a chance to explain yourself or your explanation is misinterpreted, you are left to deal with the remains. We have a desire to be vindicated, but really that's God's job to do. Waiting for vindication can be awful, but God is definitely perfect in His timing when it comes to being vindicated.

- **Judgement and criticism**
This is possibly the area leaders and pastors struggle with the most. People can be brutal in their judgements of you.

It's actually shocking the things people can say. I'm talking about Christians, who apparently have love and kindness in their heart. It can also be other leaders who work alongside you, or above you. Sometimes it's directly to your face, and sometimes it's behind your back which is sinful slander. Whilst feedback is important, judgement and criticism can be devastating and disabling. We aren't generally equipped to deal with criticism, and we certainly aren't equipped to deal with the level of criticism received.

- **Forgiveness and unforgiveness**
The frequency of which you will need to forgive people in ministry, is staggering. It feels pretty constant and yet, if you are going to model Christian values you just have to keep on doing it. Yes, the degree of hurt will differ, but it's all the same. Keeping your heart clear, is a prerequisite for good leadership. You will have to forgive your leaders, your colleagues, your people. And it could be anything from direct slander, to a negative tone. I'm not suggesting that there aren't times that you need to address the issues, but you will still have to forgive.

The flip side of this coin is that you will also have people who won't forgive you. Yeah, that's a hard one. No matter how much you try, there are some people who will keep attending your church and give you the cold shoulder. Forgetting that forgiveness is talked about with great weight in

> **Keeping your heart clear is a prerequisite for good leadership**

scriptures as opposed to other sins. And you have to keep fronting up, as they hold their unforgiveness toward you, as though you are still on trial for the perceived hurt you to have caused. It's a tough one.

☐ **The expectation gap**

Whether you are aware of it or not, when you start ministry you often have expectations. I don't know of anything as confusing as expectations. I say this because, expectations are rarely stated and rarely agreed upon by the other party. When you expected that your spouse pick up the laundry, but you didn't tell them...this is what I call an unstated expectation. Unfortunately, the problem with unstated expectations is that you are still holding the person or party accountable to the expectation that they don't know about. When you entered ministry whether you were aware of it or not, you had a vision. It is often wedged deep in your unconscious mind that you revert to at times when your mind may not be focused. I would call this an 'unstated vision'. You had a vision, but it was never communicated. To others or yourself. Which means you may not have had a chance to decide whether that vision was realistic or reasonable. In most cases, that vision is positive. But it's still unstated. It's even possible that your vision doesn't really align with Gods. You've just made some subconscious assumptions. As long as there is a gap between your unstated expectations and unstated vision and reality, you will be dissatisfied, frustrated and striving to fix it. That's why selfish ambition is so allusive.

Disappointment

It's impossible not to be disappointed at some point in ministry. Because in general, we expect good in our lives. We hear those abundant life messages promising that God only has good circumstances intended for us, and we forget that actually those who are most surrendered to God are facing the least positive experiences, like the persecuted church. And yet their hearts are full. Surrender to God, doesn't necessarily lead to comfortable situations. In fact, if you really call out to Jesus and mimic the words of Isaiah: *"Send me!"* or *"Choose me!"* There is a good chance that you may end up unpopular, in pain, and sacrificing lots. But you will have God. And you will have Him in a way that you would never experience Him, in a place of comfort and pleasure. So, disappointment is somewhat inevitable. Disappointment, especially when sustained and plentiful, is really hard to deal with. Because we are often unprepared for disappointment, we don't necessarily deal with it very well. In fact, sometimes we don't deal with it at all.

Disillusionment

I have to admit, I was rather surprised by disillusionment. I wasn't super-familiar with it as an emotion. I had to sit for a while and pray after first experiencing it. A while later, it dawned on me what I was experiencing. It's not just the fact that I had discovered something unexpected, it's the fact that I could be so wrong about something. Someone or something that I trusted in, that I believed in, that I'd even given my life to. That feeling where I thought I was safe, and all of a sudden

I realised the vulnerability of my job security. The sensation is one-part shock, one-part confusion. I haven't heard a lot about it, not like fear or insecurity. But it's prevalence can't be understated. Pastors will often remark at offence as a common cause of exiting church, but I would say disillusionment would also be pretty high up there for church-leavers. We ought to teach a bit more on the subject, to equip our people when it happens. Just a side note.

Sustained uncertainty

In my role as the Rehabilitation specialist prior to working in a church, I would often attract a lot of people who were experiencing symptoms and difficulties with their mental health. When staff experienced mental breakdowns, I would be consulted in the management of their situation. Having worked for large companies, it wasn't uncommon for the threat of redundancies to periodically materialise in response to budget changes and industry setbacks. When these times arrived, I would see a significant increase in the number of people visiting my office. The threat of redundancies would often hang around for months, and that sustained uncertainty was incredibly troublesome for employees. I've often heard in churches of the long periods that can ensue when the eldership or deacons are looking for a new Senior Minister or Senior Pastor, and it can be the same kind of experience. There are general frustrations with not being able to move forward with certain projects, but the sustained uncertainty regarding job role is enough to rattle pastors and leaders. If it's sustained for long enough, it can turn into full blown discouragement.

Sustained uncertainty can pertain to anything that people are waiting for. Were you promised a job promotion that you are still waiting for? Were you promised a pay rise? Were you told you were going to be awarded your pastor's accreditation? Well, you're better off not promising people anything, if you aren't going to do it in a reasonable timeframe, lest discouragement settle in.

One good thing

It wouldn't seem like there would be any good that comes from discouragement, but there is one thing. Discouragement forces you to count the cost of ministry. It is a big cost, and it's worth it if you know and are willing to grow through the challenge's ministry throws at you. But otherwise, it's important to take stock of what ministry really means for you.

For me, ministry means that I will have to constantly war against the flesh's desire toward significance, pride and power. It means I will have to say no to the offerings of the world that others may not have to, because there is more at stake for me. It means that I will have to give grace constantly, because I want to be a leader who models love. It means I will have to hold my tongue and reserve my own desires for the sake of unity. In the face of contempt and accusation, I will often have to choose silence and resist the desire to defend. I will have to put up with that look that non-believers give you at parties, when you tell them what you do for a living. I'll have to endure the embarrassment and shame my family has toward me being a pastor, and still return love and honour regardless. When someone comes along who is rude and condemning, I will have to forgive. I accept the betrayal, the disappointment, the judgement and criticism that comes my way all for God's glory. I may not like it, but I realise that is what I am signing up for. I am committing hour upon hour to people who may leave, who may fall away, who may sin and hurt people I love, all because I am a servant regardless of the outcome. I am acknowledging that not everyone is going to be thrilled about me being a leader. But I will have to let go, because ultimately they are simply trying to do the same thing that I am: serve God and be submitted to His Word. I presume that I will have to walk the tightrope of parenting and leading, all the while knowing that others are judging me for how my daughter turns out...and yet I will still unconditionally love her and allow her to grow and make mistakes. I am committing to doing the best for those I lead. I am committing to the fact that even though the standard is so high, I will fail frequently. But for the sake of those whom I lead, I have to pick myself up quickly and keep going. I am an instrument of reconciliation in every given situation, including those who hurt or harm me.

Counting the cost, means that I will have to follow the precepts of the Christian faith over listening to my emotions. And that's just the tip of the iceberg. I will endure the attacks of the enemy, which come more often than we would like to admit. When I count the cost, it means that I pray and battle in the spiritual realm for my community. I don't get the liberty to switch off from being a leader, even if I'm not employed. It was never the title that gave me influence. Which means, I am a leader for life. That's another cost. I know, with absolute certainty, that I will epitomise the counter-cultural values found in scripture and through the life of Christ who I am focused on becoming like. I say no to distractions, to counterfeits, to temptations. It means I will have to do all the things that God wants all believers to do, but presume that I have an audience who is watching me even when I am not aware.

It is a high call, and discouragement can force you to truly consider it, for the good and the bad. But at least when you have considered it all, you know that you know that you are willing.

What to do?
- **Acknowledge it**
Funny thing about humans. We have this strange affinity for denial, even though it serves us poorly. When you are discouraged the best thing, you can do is acknowledge it, and embrace the subsequent sorrow that follows such an admission. It's not going to go away as long as you are denying it, anyway. Second to this:

    - **Conduct a thorough assessment of your life**
    When things got really bad, I drew up for myself a table in which I listed every area of my life that I was disappointed with. I then identified where there might have been some unstated expectations. I also noted if there were any faulty beliefs. I then wrote in the final column the truth that God wanted me to know. It really helped. I was able to return to that table a few times, and keep pursuing healing. It was empowering!

- **Look for a quick win**
Joshua and the Israelites had just observed one of the most epic battles in history. They had walked around the walls

of Jericho seven times, and at their shouts the walls came crashing down allowing them to enter the city and conquer it. However, only one chapter later in Joshua 7, we are being shown that one of the Israelites, despite the incredible events of that day, decided to sin and take items that they weren't meant to. This attracted the Lord's anger. All of a sudden there was question over future military success. Joshua, distraught, seeks God who tells Him of the sin in the camp. God asks Joshua to gather the people, to reveal the culprit. The Israelites stone and burn him and all his possessions. And the Lord's anger is subdued. What a miserable day for the Israelites?! Especially Joshua. The awesome thing about God, is that in the next chapter (Joshua 8:1) He says to Joshua: *"Do not be discouraged"*, and proceeds to outlay the next attack in which success is promised. He didn't allow Joshua the time to sit in the discouragement, He arranged a quick win. God knows that we need a win sometimes. We just need the encouragement that victory brings, even when its largely His doing. One of the best pieces of advice I can give you, is look for those simple and small opportunities for a quick win and ask God to bring you success. It will lift your spirits. Implement something that you've been putting off. Even if it's as simple as clearing up your storage area. Do something. One task I used to do periodically, was clean and re-organise my desk. I would even go to the local office supplies store and get myself some new folders and stationery, that would support my desire to get focused. It always felt like I was getting somewhere. It would kickstart that momentum, that was being threatened by discouragement.

☐ Confidence in God

Steven Furtick[18] has a brilliant message about how we aren't meant to have confidence in ourselves, we are meant to have confidence in God. He bases this message on Philippians 3, where Paul is talking about having no confidence in the flesh and perceiving his many outwardly righteous accomplishments as rubbish. I am not even going to try and better what he is done. Go check out the message. I simply say this, our confidence is not supposed to be man-made. It's supposed to be in God.

☐ Enlist new members and don't limit them

If you are stagnating as a result of discouragement, the best thing you could possibly do is enlist some excited and passionate fresh new members. Give them some responsibility, give them a bit of leash. Don't limit them. Recognise that your desires to limit may be coming from cynicism and discouragement. And when they succeed, don't feel threatened by it. Allow the success to excite you, allow yourself to start believing again. Often we limit new additions to a team or group, because we are fearful to protect the dynamics we have. However, my experience is that if you wisely choose leaders and engage them at the right time, it can be the best step toward progress. They can improve or enhance the dynamics. So, don't rely on yourself to summons the energy to do something new, enlist and release another. You'll be a great leader for having equipped and released a good team member as well. Or promote a faithful person. Give them a new opportunity and more influence.

YOU WILL GET DISCOURAGED

☐ **Remind yourself that faith isn't an emotion**
Sometimes we act like faith is an emotion. But it's really not. You know those times you are praying for someone to be healed, and you try to clear your head and switch on the faith button that is supposed to make you feel faithful. You figure if you feel that faith surging, it might actually happen. Well, faith is actually not an emotion at all. It's a belief and a choice. When I had my earliest sign of depression, I found myself in bed one-night praying. I had this feeling of heaviness, and I didn't really know why. I obviously know now, it was the first-time discouragement appeared. I remember clearly saying to God, "God I don't know what this is. I don't know why this feeling is here in my heart. But I know you do. God I put my faith in you today, that you will bring understanding about this feeling or that you will heal me. Even though I still feel it right now, I chose to acknowledge it, but I also chose to believe you will deliver me from it". I went to sleep that night, with that feeling still in my heart. But my mind was clear - I was trusting God with it. I didn't expect an immediate change. I didn't try to manufacture a faith feeling. I just believed. By the next day it had subsided significantly. I was pleased that I didn't let the feeling envelope me and rob me of my belief. Faith is not a feeling, you chose to put your faith in Him because you know Him, and you believe Him. If that feels like too much right now, take more time to really get to know Him. We affirm the goodness of God, when we know His goodness.

☐ **Get advice**
Talk to someone. Talk to other people about how they have

dealt with feelings of discouragement. We've all had our fair share.

- **Take on a project that you'd be excited about**
This doesn't promise to resolve those deep discouragements that have been hanging around for a while. It does, however, remind you that there is still fun to be had. That it's not the end of the world, if life isn't great in certain areas. For me, our Internship program was that. Whilst I never fully took it on, I took some time aside to make recommendations and conduct research on the Internship program and ways we could rehash it. It was so much fun! Maybe your project is outside of ministry. A fellow pastor once told me that after a significant discouragement, he took on some renovations to his home. It not only distracted him, but it gave him something to invest into. So have a think, what is a project that you could do that would get you excited again?

- **Look for inspiration**
Mother Teresa has got to be one of the most inspiring human beings. When there are times that I have been discouraged, I've checked out some of the quotes or stories about her. What an inspiration! Talk about someone who had great perspective. She knew what was important, and she sacrificed herself to serve the poor. In one story I read, she walked into the slums and lived with the people, at times experiencing life through their eyes including having no food, or money, and having to beg. Even though she could have walked back to the convent at any time and received lodging, food, money

and employment. And there are plenty more people out there, that help you put the matters of life into perspective. Find those stories. Read them. Let them encourage you.

☐ **Resolve the dissonance**
We aren't usually this self-aware, but sometimes the reason we are discouraged or can't get out of discouragement is because of unresolved internal conflicts. Sometimes we have conflicting desires. Sometimes we have conflicting beliefs. Other times we can have conflicting values. Amazingly, our minds can often hold two opposing ideas completely unaware of the fact that these two ideas contradict each other. Unfortunately, they usually don't live peacefully alongside each other. The aftermath of such conflict is stress, anxiety and restlessness. There are plenty of internal conflicts that are triggered by scripture. The idea that God is

> Our **confidence** is not supposed to be **man-made**

loving, and confronting the God of the Old Testament who often appears unloving is probably one of the most common internal conflicts I hear from other Christians. The kind of internal conflicts that may exist in leaders though, is believing that you need to be strong while not ever feeling strong at all. Or feeling the pressure to perform, when you are more concerned about factors that don't improve performance. Even the internal conflict between playing the long game, when you are being told you need to demonstrate some success immediately. Simple things like believing you are free and desiring freedom, but being crippled by others' opinions of you. Or it can be as small as wanting to eat the cookie, but knowing you shouldn't eat the cookie. The obvious example is when Paul says that *"For what I want to do I do not do, but what I hate I do."* Romans 7:15. This is a classic internal conflict expending way more energy than we can imagine. It is exhausting to fight against the flesh, or be in a battle to resolve unrealistic expectations that conflict with the life we want. Perfectionism is an internal conflict. I've never met a person who is satisfied with the effect perfectionism has on their lifestyle and relationships. Whatever, your specific internal conflict, do your best to resolve it. You will live much lighter and you won't be such an easy prey for discouragement.

☐ **Counselling**
As always, seek some help. Some things are a no-brainer. If you have had any suicidal thoughts, stop reading and get help now. If the discouragement has weighed quite heavily on you, to the point that you don't recognise yourself, just get counselling. Don't be tempted to make judgements about yourself for pursuing counselling. You aren't crazy! The mind and heart are like a car, they may need a tune up. They need to clear out the old residual materials that are stopping it from working at its optimum. Don't listen to others judgement about counselling. I was a counsellor, and it's so unfortunate that there is a stigma around it. In my opinion, a counsellor is a really professional friend skilled in the art of good questions and observations. I often got told that counselling was rubbish by other Christians, it was very hard not to take offence to that. I couldn't disagree more. When I trained to be a counsellor, I

signed up based on a Word from God. Every client I met with, were prayed for by me. I was relying on the Holy Spirit in every counselling session. Let me tell you, I saw breakthroughs in people's lives who weren't believers.

The question is not whether something is wrong or right, it's whether God can work through it...and I know He can, because I've seen Him do it time and again. If you are worried, go see a Christian counsellor. Don't be a hero, just get help.

Final thoughts...

I've had allergies to dust-mites and certain pollens ever since I was a kid. The hay fever used to get so severe, that my doctor eventually prescribed a treatment called systematic desensitisation which involved regular injections. I've lived with these allergies for so long, that I can predict with absolute precision when my hay fever is about to kick in. It's like clockwork. As soon as I sense it, I activate a program that I devised some time ago to minimise the effect. I am prepared and I know exactly what to do.

If discouragement is so common and close to guaranteed, is it possible to be better prepared for it? We don't think this way, because we prefer to be hardship-avoidant. But is it not wise to have a plan, like my allergy plan, rather than live in ignorance? I don't have any specific thoughts yet on exactly what those preventative measures could be, but suffice to say that it would be wise to consider the specific causes of your discouragement and make a plan for how you can respond when they come about. Not everything is predictable in life, but for those factors that are it would be worth making a plan.

The Jesus factor

Jesus didn't just get tempted to be discouraged, he was discouraged. Mark 14:34 says:

> *"My soul is overwhelmed with sorrow to the point of death," he said to them. "Stay here and keep watch."*

There are so many layers to this statement that shocks me. *'Sorrow to the point of death'*? That's a heavy sorrow. So, Christ was actually that down? That disheartened? Apparently so.

Another shocking part about this situation, is the fact that He tells the disciples. The people He is leading. He doesn't tell them all the details, but He certainly doesn't hide his emotions. There have been many times that I have been told by well-meaning leaders to take a vow of silence. We should hide our struggles and pain. Well, Jesus didn't. He was authentic. And vulnerable. Doesn't it just make you love Jesus all the more? He didn't invite them into the struggle, he took it to His Father. But He certainly didn't deceive them about how He was feeling.

So, can we all relax a bit now? That tendency to hide our emotions, and pretend we don't struggle…that need to appear joyful, even when we are down…you don't have to do that anymore. You can be real, authentic and vulnerable. You don't have to invite everyone into the specifics…take them to the Father and a select few friends…but you don't have to pretend you have it all together. Being discouraged does not reflect on your ability to lead. It's not even about your ability anyway. You are called. That's all you need to know sometimes. Jesus wills that you are here, not your competency. Your competency helps, so never stop growing. But ultimately you are doing what you

YOU WILL GET DISCOURAGED

are doing because He wills it. So, relax. You don't have to prove anything. You don't have to feel ashamed.

CHAPTER 8

There's never enough...

I've recently become really addicted to a game on my iPhone. It's called Cooking Craze. I love it. I got my sister-in-law hooked on it as well. I've 'travelled' through New York, Paris, Italy, and I'm almost finished Bangkok. The next level will be Japan. I can't wait to see the type of food I will have to prepare there. I'm a little frustrated at the moment though, because I can't seem to get passed this level in Bangkok. I make Tom Yum Soup, Chilli Crab and Pad Thai. I've literally mastered it, and I'm super-fast. But in this last level, I frequently run out of time.

I have to serve about 28 dishes in 60 seconds. Every time that buzzer goes, I still have another five dishes to go. There's just never enough time. I don't know how anyone is finishing this level. I can't actually progress to Tokyo, until I finish it either. Ugh! So frustrating! I've wasted so many lives, and spent so many hours… and I'm adamant not to pay money for bonus features that would no doubt help me pass it…

Being a bit of a visionary, I find it so hard to keep going with what I am doing when my mind is already planning the future. It was the same with ministry. I always had some new project or initiative I had dreamed up, that in my imagination would be revolutionary. But so often, I just couldn't get through one major hurdle. I would feel stuck and unable to move. That's so disabling for dreamers like me. And the major hurdle was resources, or lack of them. Whether it be the people, equipment, financial resources, time or programs...it never felt like there was enough of anything to take action.

Working for a big church is deceiving. I thought that they would have more disposable income, but they generally don't. They have the same challenges as anywhere else when it comes to resources...it never feels like you have enough. For some this might be just an annoyance...but for others, it really gets you down. So, for this reason I think a lack of resources is worthy of discussion.

Emails you would rather not open

After I produced the Christmas Production, it was a few weeks until the office closed. My whole focus was to catch up on eight weeks of Connect Group work. Despite having to largely neglect Connect Groups for that time, I had at least made contact with new people who had submitted queries and had preliminary discussions about groups. I just hadn't been able to place them, and the saving grace was that our groups would close over the Christmas break.

I returned in January to start placing people in groups, and really hit the ground running. Unfortunately, I experienced a terrible blow...In the first few days, I received two reply emails. The

> We want to make an **impact.** That implies that we need to be doing **more** than we are now.

first one was a couple that were so appalled at the time it had taken to get into a group, that they had decided to move onto another church. The second email was a response from a person who had re-committed her life to faith, that figured because it had taken so long to get into a group, that it must have been a sign that faith was not for her. I was crushed! I was devastated! I told my Pastor about it and he was notably disappointed, but he didn't have a go at me. I think he could see that I was making myself pay for it enough. But largely nobody else knew. I couldn't imagine how I could win. If I had dropped the ball with the Christmas Production I would have let more people down. The trade-off was potentially a person not continuing with their faith and a couple who left our church. I couldn't figure out how I could have done anything different to change the outcome. I had no people to delegate the task to, and I was already working ridiculous hours to do the Christmas Production.

    I prayed and talked to God, and reasserted a mantra I often told myself in previous workplaces. I reminded myself that I am not responsible for the available resources, whether it be personnel or money. I do the best I can with what I am given, but if after that I still can't get it done...? It's actually an issue for those above me to resolve. Even though I would constantly be trying to engage volunteers to do some hours in the office, they were often short lived. I put proposals in to get more staff, but it would usually eventuate with a person doing four hours in the department a week, who was also primarily engaged in another department. Connect Groups would get 'parked' when they had something significant going on in their ministry. And at the end of the day, I was the one who had to face the disappointment of the people if services weren't delivered as they expected. It used to bug me to no end when other pastors would come and say, "Jack still hasn't been placed in a group. Could you please get onto that asap?" It was really hard to not get defensive. There were heaps of others who hadn't been placed either. I could only do so much, including the work I took home. It was so annoying that they acted like it was my fault, that I had been under-resourced for my job. As if I didn't feel awful enough that I was in a situation where I largely couldn't resolve the long-term issue, and knew that if an event was around the corner I was going to continue to disappoint someone. So, I just had to settle it in my spirit that I was setup to disappoint people, and learn how to prevent that feeling from entering my heart.

Equations...

I would hazard a guess that you understand what I mean when I say, "there's never enough". In ministry, it usually manifests as not having enough time, money, space, people, and volunteers. The logic goes like this:

More money = more time = more volunteers = more people

OR

More volunteers = more time = more people

OR

More money = more space = more time = more volunteers

OR

More people = more money = more volunteers = more time = more people

We could go on and on, because we largely believe that more of ANYTHING usually means we can invest in more of something else. It's a domino effect. I can see why we are so busy, we are always chasing more. Here is a brief list of all the 'mores' most churches are running after:

- More missions giving
- More tithes
- More staff
- More community engagement or community outreach departments
- More missional activities
- More salvations
- More men's stuff
- More women's stuff
- More family stuff
- More stuff for business people
- More leaders and volunteers
    - For Kids Ministry
    - For Connect Groups
    - For Worship: drummers, bassists, stage managers, cameras etc.
    - For Men's Ministry
    - For Women's Ministry
    - For Sunday teams
    - For Major events
    - For catering: tea and coffee

- More Prayer team
  - For Youth
  - For Young Adults
- More space or more buildings
- More services
- More cultural engagement
- More new people processes
- More new Christians processes
- More discipleship programs
- More evangelists
- More prophetic people

Of course, none of the above are bad. I'm just noting the vast number of areas in which we are often desiring to grow and consequently experience lack. I can't say I've ever heard of a church that wants less. It's just counterintuitive to how we work. We are visionaries. We want to make an impact. That implies that we need to be doing more than we are now, to get to the places we haven't arrived at yet.

Here's the thing…I often find that church leaders are the most unhealthily dissatisfied bunch of people I've ever met. They get excited about momentum, but they are rarely happy about where their ministries are at. Now maybe that's just the way it is when you are a visionary, but I know it's not really healthy for the mind to sustain such a constant sense of incompletion. The whole time I was in ministry, it never changed. There were very few moments when you were completely satisfied with how something turned out.

What does it look like?

So, what are the signs that you are frustrated by never having enough?

- **You're doing more than you should**
  When you are in a place of constant need in ministry, there is only so long you can live like that before you start to think you have to do something directly. Depending on what department you are in, there is often a limitation on your actions. That doesn't mean that you don't look for opportunities, but it's just a reality. Let me give you an example. When I was working in the Connect Group department, I would frequently have people telling me that they didn't feel connected. Sometimes they had tried, and sometimes they hadn't. I knew that their assessment was probably true, because I had experienced it myself. But we just didn't have enough people stepping up to lead groups. It was a cultural problem that I knew would take a while to address. So, in the meantime, I ended up with three Connect Groups. I had my normal group that I had been running from the beginning, I had a families group and I had a Creative Connect Group. You can imagine how long that lasted! I dropped the Creative Connect Group not long after, and the families group several months later. Whilst I was the Connect Group Pastor, connection was a church wide issue. But for some reason I thought I could change that by just starting more groups. Not my smartest moment of course. If you start to think that you have got to just get in there and do the stuff that you really need a team of leaders to do? Then you've probably reaching a point of conundrum over the

'there's never enough' mindset. And if you keep going that way, it will either be a cap on real growth, or you'll burn out. Or you start to try and fix matters that are outside of your control.

- **You're frustrated**
You know that feeling...it's when you feel irritated, limited, stuck, exasperated. It causes you to be easily angered, and more distracted. I can remember going to a counsellor at some point in my tenure, and saying "Why do I feel frustrated ALL THE TIME?" The counsellor was so quick to respond, "It's a symptom of blocked goals". Wow, he couldn't have been more correct. That's exactly what it felt like. Everywhere I looked there was a barrier to what I wanted to do, where I wanted to take the ministry or even where I wanted to be as a leader and pastor. I felt like I wasn't seeing any joy in any aspect of ministry. I think my frustration lasted about two years. It's not fun to be frustrated. You may be surprised to learn also that frustration is believed to have an impact on your body. Not to mention the impact on relationships. Have a think about it...how often do you feel frustrated? Over it? Annoyed? You may have reached your limit with 'there never being enough' mindset

- **You feel like you can't rest**
The number of times I got into the habit of working all day, coming home and doing the family routine, and sitting with a laptop in front of the TV doing more work...it was pretty bad. Because it just never felt like there was ever enough time in the day. There probably wasn't really. It wasn't just that.

Sometimes I found that it wasn't a particularly busy season, but I would still sit on the couch with the laptop at night. It wasn't until my daughter started Prep, and I had my days off entirely to myself that I realised I just didn't know how to rest anymore. That isn't an issue I had dealt with prior to working in ministry. I would go out, go shopping, go for a swim, read a book. But somehow I had become convinced that maybe I would be able to plough through those barriers if I just put more time in. I just needed to do more, and I would have the results I wanted. It wasn't really true. I know activity doesn't necessarily equal success. But I had just become so ingrained in this 'never enough' mindset that I didn't notice the creeping belief…that maybe I wasn't enough…and maybe God isn't enough. That mindset is a breeding ground for restlessness.

- **You feel overwhelmed frequently**

    If you sustain that feeling of being overwhelmed for long enough, it's likely to become something much more sinister. I had learnt to pause when I was overwhelmed, because I knew that an unhealthy perspective is detrimental to your work. But it was pretty hard not to feel overwhelmed when I got those emails that reminded me of how I or the ministry was falling short. What about all the programs or initiatives you want to start but don't have the resources, engagement or time to do? Overwhelmed. What about all the times you are tied up in meetings and you can't get any desk time? Overwhelmed. What about all the people that you know you have to meet with but can't find a window? Overwhelmed. What about all those people who threaten leaving because of not feeling connected? Overwhelmed. The feeling of being

overwhelmed, is the one factor that makes me think that being a pastor is 98% a mind and heart game. If you can manage your thought life, and your heart, you are winning.

- **You don't really enjoy any of your successes**
When you are so aware of the need, it's pretty hard to rejoice in the successes. When I had 47 groups in a church of 1000, my sense of satisfaction was not increased when we reached 60. Even though it was progress. Truth is, once I reached 75 groups, that became my 'holy' number. Nothing was good enough if it wasn't 75. And even when we were at 75, I still wanted to be at 120. We aren't wrong for having goals and targets. I suppose I am just shedding light on the fact that successes and progress should be celebrated. Yet, when you are focused on the gap it's really hard to care about progress.

Faith and function

A congregation member was chatting with me about a relationship they were about to get into. They had dated the person before, and it didn't exactly work out the first time. And now that they were contemplating doing it again. It was bringing to the surface a whole bunch of anxiety. I can remember exhorting them to take one step at a time, trust in God and lift their faith. That this was an opportunity to grow in their faith in Jesus. It's so funny how we are lavish with advice, that we don't really listen to ourselves. Ministry is 100% an exercise in trusting God, taking one step at a time and lifting your faith. But for some reason we separate such spiritual principles from our own ministry experience. As though God is primarily concerned with how we minister to others, and not at all concerned about our own faith journey in the midst of ministry. It's all an opportunity to become more mature, more surrendered and more Christ-like. Now there's some 'mores' we can really be interested in.

A gap between the vision and the present is good

The mistake we make is, forgetting that FAITH is meant to fill the gap. Instead, out of panic and pressure, we rely on human competencies only to see that vision come to pass. Or we give up on the vision. Or we presume vision is overrated.

How wrong could we be? In the gap where we have placed extreme striving and overwork, nestled neatly, instead should be prayer and supplication. And diligent action. Not overwork.

Poor foundations

I'm sure you've all heard of a 'poor mentality' or 'poverty mentality'. A poor mentality suggests that the way in which you think about money, has a great influence on how you use it. Often if you've come from an upbringing where money was scarce, you can adopt a poor mentality because you've come to permanently believe that money will always be scarce. The outcome may be that you spend money as soon as you get it. You don't make plans to address your finances. You blame others for your situation. And you've largely just assumed that you will be 'poor' for the rest of your life.

The worst part about a poor mentality is the fact that you are constantly making decisions from a basis of lack. And lack is a terrible foundation for decision making. Think about it. When you are lacking love, what will you do to get it? Make a bad choice in a partner? Endure an abusive relationship because it's better than being alone?

The same applies to feeling like you don't have enough in ministry. Whether it's money, people, space or time. Feeling like you are lacking, is not a great place from which to try and build a ministry. If you are lacking people resources, you might be too pushy with your recruitment and risk forever losing someone. If you are lacking money, you might preach a bit too much about money at your Sunday services, and risk alienating the new non-Christian who was already suspicious about church. If you are lacking space, you might get possessive of rooms and justify the raucous argument you are about to have with the other ministry leader who claimed the space first. And if you are lacking time, you might use your power to misuse your administrator or just take way too much work home each night.

Now this doesn't negate that often you don't have enough leaders or money. Our lack is often very real, and you know it is because you experience the practical consequence of that lack. So, I'm not suggesting you deny the reality. I'm more saying that you resist the temptation to accommodate a mindset of lack in how you manage your ministry, and in place of it activate faith. If you don't have the faith for it anymore, seek out some intercessors in your church and ask them to pray. They are all too happy to partner in prayer.

I would argue that it's better to do less and focus more, than to adopt this lack mentality. Sometimes we are so reluctant to stop some of the initiatives we are doing, and so we live in that realm of not wanting

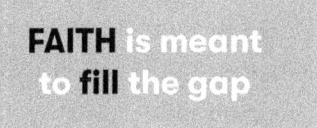

FAITH is meant to fill the gap

to disappoint people who like the initiative and denying that you don't have the resources to keep it up. That will probably lead to unnecessary stress and a lack mentality. I think the lack mentality is way worse than stopping something you were doing.

I often think "what would a church plant consider critical in the start-up phase?" Because people get saved at church plants and small churches and they are discipled. They achieve all that big churches achieve on smaller budgets and with less resources. Ask yourself, what is a non-negotiable for the growth of this church? You may actually focus your resourcing and start to think a bit more creatively about what you do have at hand.

"I can do all things..." Philippians 4:13

No, I won't be telling you how you can do all things through Christ who strengthens you. I won't be telling you that you should just keep going, and God will provide. Because I actually can't. There are enough churches that close these days to demonstrate that the longevity of a church is not a guarantee. That passage has obviously been grossly misused.

The context for that verse is the theme of **contentment**. What a word. I love it, and I hate it all at the same time. Because I feel like I was born with discontentment, and I have worked a lifetime to try and be rid of it, and I'm still not there. I simultaneously desire it, because I know I would experience so much peace and joy if I had it.

In this highly quoted passage, Paul is expressing the fact that Christ gives him the strength to be content in every circumstance. Whether he has only a little, or plenty. Cool. But just think about this staggering underlying fact for a moment; Paul, the apostle, the evangelist, and church planter was UNDER-resourced. That is what this passage proves. Paul was the most influential person in the establishment of the church, besides Jesus. And yet he was under-resourced and was content regardless. Based on Paul's comments, doesn't it stand to reason that it is normal to be under-resourced at times in ministry, regardless of how good you are? Isn't it possible that we can be content like Paul? Paul was in prison, and could have very easily given up and figured that his ministry had come to an end. Instead, he sends these epic letters and uses the one influence he has left, his writing, to keep his mission going. There are times when accepting where you are in ministry, whether rich or poor, will lead you to reflect on the range of options that are actually available to you right now. Just like Paul accepted he was in prison, but found a way to keep encouraging the Body. Often in ministry we can be so focused on what we aren't doing, and what we don't have and how much growth isn't happening, that we miss the opportunities to engage in that which is happening now that we can enhance and invest in. Often they are the areas God is really moving in, and wants us to jump on board. Often those areas are the ones that will build the infrastructure to sustain any future growth.

I can remember when our Connect group numbers hit rock bottom, I was pretty down about it. I was praying about it one day, and I felt a peace in my heart that God was saying that the numbers were exactly where they needed to be right now. Naturally, my follow up question was "Well, if this is the case, what am I supposed to be doing now?" I knew the answer. I had to build my leadership team, strengthen its focus, structure it for sustained growth and invest in the leaders. So, I started focusing on leadership development, and establishing a team that would stabilise the future for all newcomers. I also started to ask myself the bigger questions: What will facilitate future connection? It was then that I started looking at these short-term groups, that would pave the way for longer term connections and identifying leaders. All of this came from accepting that the low number of groups was where we were meant to be, and instead seeing it as an opportunity. After that, we grew to 75 groups within one year.

Accepting where you are at, doesn't mean you are giving up. It means you are acknowledging reality. And reality is a great place from which to start strategising.

However, there are times you are meant to be unsettled, as a motivator for change. There is a tension between having vision and pursuing that, and being content and grateful with where you are. I don't know exactly how that tension works, and I certainly don't understand when each is appropriate. I wish I had worked out the science of it to share it with you now. But I think, once again, this is where discernment kicks in. Being able to know the times, is a great skill and the height of wisdom. So, if you are discontent all the time in ministry, it's possible you see a lot of life through that lens. If that's the case, the solution is to seek help and seek God. But ultimately long-term discontentment psychologically and emotionally doesn't lead to anything positive. Also, discontentment is so closely related to ungratefulness, which surely is not a great way to approach ministry or God who has provided all you have.

Solution time

Alright, so here are my thoughts on actions you can take to grow and manage this challenge:

THERE'S NEVER ENOUGH...

- **Pray and seek God**
  The first place of action is to seek God and pray. Bring ministry needs to Him, before you even contemplate how you are going to fix the problems. I am sometimes a little surprised at how few ministry leaders pray for their ministries. I was guilty of this for a time too. It sounds counterintuitive right? Well, you go ahead and battle this in the spiritual realm. And when you do, pray with confidence and faith that God will deliver on your request. Remember that he probably wants it as much as you, so pray like you know that.

- **Focus**
  Consider whether this may be an opportunity to focus and consolidate your efforts. So frequently, we can adopt activities and initiatives that aren't really adding any value to our ministry. Somewhere along the line they may have, and so you keep doing it not realising that it's now obsolete. When you are under-resourced, it is a good time to review all of what you do and consider the necessity of each activity. Maybe it is more time consuming than it needs to be. When I first started in Connect Groups, we were individually placing every person into a group. It was intended to give the personal touch. Several years in, I realised that this process, was limiting the capability of our team. We had one person doing a full four hours on this every week. So, I then started investigating a database that would allow people to browse our groups and connect the person to the leader, cutting out the middleman. The outcome would be a reduction of four hours labour to the ministry each week. Makes sense right? But often leaders

don't take the time to review how they complete their tasks, and miss opportunities for cutting off the fat, in terms of processes, roles and systems. Maybe this time of being under-resourced is a time to review and consolidate. You may be surprised to find that the stewardship of your resources can be drastically improved.

- **Remind yourself that you aren't a customer service officer**
  There are a lot of 'never enough's' that we feel, that have come directly from our church members complaints. Just be careful not to get sucked into those conversations, or at least be careful not to let it into your heart. Often the people who are complaining about where there is lack won't put their hands up to help resolve it. So, what was the point of their complaint? Well, the fact is we aren't customer service officers, and we aren't there to please every person and their individual issues with the church. We know that, but often when we do get a complaint we still try organisationally to resolve it. Some complaints are not detrimental to the life, health and growth of the church.

- **Ask the broader questions and make a plan**
  This is a great opportunity to reflect on the broader themes and conversations pertinent to ministry. Here are some examples of questions that may help you:
    - What is the greatest investment of my time?
    - What are the activities that only I can do?
    - What activities will reap the greatest rewards to the whole church, if I were to implement it now?

- What activities will invest in the future stability and growth of the church and the ministry?
- What areas are critical for growth right now?
- What is important now, that I can I focus on, that will be hard to focus on when it grows?
- What's not working, or a waste of time, that we can cull?
- Which leaders can I focus on developing?
- What leaders are time consuming and distracting us from our vision?
- Which leader is so influential that if I were to develop them, would multiply my influence or the values of the ministry?

Once you've answered those questions, and whatever other ones you come up with, make a plan. Even if it is just two objectives that you can invest in now that will pay dividends in the future. Not only will it probably be more effective than trying to do everything, it will get your mind off what you don't have.

- **Look at what you have**
  Make a list of all that is going well, that you are grateful for. Even in the worst of circumstances, there is so much to be grateful for. Be grateful that you are called, and that you know where God wants you to be. Be grateful for the leaders you do have. For the money you do receive. Gratefulness and joy are so closely related. If you want more joy, start by being grateful.

The Jesus factor

I can't recall a single place in which Jesus suggests that He is discontent with what He has. For three years, He seemed fairly satisfied to have mainly 12 disciples and a number of committed followers. He wasn't trying to do a massive expansion, He was primarily focused on the twelve. Even when only a few fish and small loaves were presented to Him to feed the masses, He didn't say it wasn't enough. He miraculously made the fish and loaves enough, and all were satisfied. We might not be able to do miracles, but we certainly know someone who can and who frequently maximises every resource. If you only care to observe His mighty hand frequently at work.

We are not in lack, when we have Jesus. The Psalmist reminds us, that when the Lord is our Shepherd, we lack nothing (Psalm 23). And Christ is the Good Shepherd.

CHAPTER 9

The enemy will attack you

When we were kids, my younger cousin who is about four years younger than me, used to be picked on by my brother and an older cousin. I was often left out of such games, being a girl. I was happy enough to watch the mayhem from the sidelines. But my younger cousin wasn't so lucky. There was one game they created that would be played at an aunties' house. They had a long open lounge area that the adults would not frequent. My brother and older cousin would hide in the open lounge, and my younger cousin would have to wait in the study at the other end of the lounge area. Once they were hidden, he would have to come out and withstand the barrage of pillows and ottomans pelted at him and make it to the end of the room. They were pretty aggressive at times, but he largely took it in his stride because the thrill was in the surprise attack. He would be laughing and smiling in anticipation. And of course, once they emerged he would be hysterically entertained, and the adrenaline would kick in as he attempted to escape. Sometimes it would go too far, and he would get hurt. That's when they invented 'magic'. They told him they had magic hands and would 'heal' him.

> **Our battle isn't with each other.**

Talk about a placebo! He would buy it, and would be up and ready for the next run in a matter of seconds. It was all pretty amusing.

Real attacks aren't so amusing. Especially when the enemy is involved. He isn't interested in fun or excitement. His main agenda is to hurt us. The enemy attacks everyone and ministry is no exception. In fact, I found that the attacks were probably worse in ministry. But that's not to say that it always is. That's just my experience. But it's guaranteed, he will attack you. And you can become weary and tired.

Happy Easter

The Easter services were looking very promising. We had been coordinating a handful of performers and script writers to present a dramatic piece involving dance and drama. I hadn't really been involved in anything quite like it. The scene was portraying a woman in the midst of warring thoughts, as spoken by two demonic personalities. They were tempting her, condemning her, all the while coaxing her into a tempestuous dance. At the end she leaps into the arms of Jesus. It was very powerful and moving. We knew it was going to have an impact, we could just feel it. I was in charge of bringing it all together, which was at times proving difficult. But even though there were some delays on the components, I was confident that it would all be good if I just kept trusting in Him. So, a few nights before as I put my head down to sleep I found myself drifting off into dreamland quietly settled and worry-free. Only, as I drifted into that semi-sleeping and semi-conscious state I could feel hands strangling me around the throat and someone sitting over me. I couldn't breathe or speak! It was absolutely terrifying. I somehow managed to sit

THE ENEMY WILL ATTACK YOU

up and push the person off whilst simultaneously screaming "IN JESUS NAME!". It felt so real. I don't even fully know if it was a dream or reality. It's possible it was all taking place in the spirit realm. Either way, it was the first time something like that had ever happened to me. When I came back to the office the next day, it turned out that my boss' family had the same unsettled sleep. We committed to praying for each other throughout the week. But it certainly wouldn't be the end of the attacks.

How bad does it get?

Spiritual attacks can get pretty bad. My experience is that some people call everything a spiritual attack, and others will look to explain unusual scenarios, with everything but 'spiritual attack'. But if we are to believe scripture we know that they do happen. And if we believe scripture we know that sometimes it's the flesh. Often they are both!

Spiritual attacks can come in a variety of ways. Sometimes they are obvious, just like my experience. Or sometimes they are subtle, through relationships, pride, temptation and other areas that are much harder to detect. I would say that the subtle stuff is worse, since it has more room for influence and less likely to be quickly restrained. The obvious stuff can be a bit full on. It is obvious, and therefore, you wisen up to the ploy pretty quickly even if you are terrified.

Over the years, I have observed some trends about the nature of the enemy's spiritual attacks:

- **The enemy is most likely to attack with temptation**
  Leading you into sin, is one of the core focuses of the enemy.

He wants you to fail. He wants you to question whether God can really transform you. Furthermore, after you fail, he can hit you with guilt and shame. They are terrible motivators in life. I haven't seen anything reinforce a slavery mentality more than guilt and shame. When you are in ministry, there is more at stake if you sin. Well, at least if they are the obvious sins then we tend to judge more harshly. So, it's definitely on his agenda to encourage you to sin. Some sins may remove you from ministry for life, and that would certainly suit him fine.

I should also mention that whilst we have a tendency to rate and categorise sin, he doesn't. All sin is sin, with a steep slope to more sin. We tend to become more vigilant when it comes to the obvious sins, like those of financial integrity and sexual integrity. But he is just as happy that you spoke rudely to another team member, or gossiped to a congregation member. He takes pleasure in it all. I think he particularly enjoys when we deceive ourselves into thinking that we are doing well, because we aren't committing the 'big' sins.

- **He often attacks with consecutive blows**
I've noticed that when the enemy is attacking you, he will plant you with a series of hits as opposed to just one big hit. Of course, big stuff also happens. But he knows that each hit weakens us just a little bit more, making it really hard to gain strength again. It's the classic Job, of the Old Testament, scenario. First he lost the oxen and donkey. Secondly, he lost his servants and the sheep. Thirdly, he lost his camels. And of course, lastly, his sons and daughters. It's the equivalent of being punched four times, without time to recover. There may

be mainly one or two attacks that could really knock you out in one hit. But in a boxing match, smaller repeated hits can still render you knocked out. And to be knocked out, is the enemy's agenda, regardless of how it's done.

- **The enemy will often attack you when you are weak**
  The enemy is most likely to tempt you or divide you, when you are at your weakest. It's kind of obvious really…it's the time you are most likely to have your defences down. When I was at my lowest point, contemplating whether life was even worth living, I couldn't help but notice how quickly the temptations, lies and relational problems surfaced. It was the equivalent to when you are sick, and you are susceptible to other health conditions. I remember at the beginning of last year, being sick for around two weeks with three different illnesses. It was terrible! It all makes sense that the enemy would attack at such times…the likelihood of his success is higher at these times.

- **The direct attacks often happen when you're doing something good**
  I've often heard people say that the enemy only attacks you when you are doing something right. Maybe. To be honest, I think he just attacks us all the time because he hates us. What I do find, however, is that he tends to vary the type of attack based on differing scenarios. The full on, direct, spiritual force, in-your-face kind of attack like my story tends to happen when you are doing something that may have some positive impact for the greater church or kingdom. In that instance, he

knows he can't really stop you, so he just wants to scare and intimidate you. Maybe sometimes he means for it to change our plans, but I think it's more of a hateful retaliation. Like when a kid does that final lash out, after realising they are definitely not getting their way. On the other hand, he does a lot of his subtle work when life is going 'well'. That's when temptations like pride are most likely to settle in. Of course, there isn't any real 'set in stone' approach, this is simply a tendency that I've observed.

You might have your own observations, and you should certainly take note, because chances are he is going to use them again.

Magic tricks

My husband Josh went through this stage recently of being rather obsessed with magic tricks. It all began when he discovered the Penn & Teller show. He was watching it so much! I gave him a special deck of trick cards for his birthday. He loved it! So now, he primarily entertains kids, either our relatives or Kids Ministry, in a non-professional capacity with his magic tricks. The grown-ups have seen it all before, and aren't exactly fooled. Especially me, who gets to watch behind the scenes as he practices for hours to nail a trick that takes a millisecond to perform.

The enemy might be cunning, but largely he uses the same tricks. It doesn't mean those tricks aren't effective, it just means that they are identifiable and sometimes predictable. 1 Corinthians 10:13 *"No temptation has overtaken you that is not common to man"* certainly suggests the same idea.

THE ENEMY WILL ATTACK YOU

In my experience, there are a few really key areas that the enemy focuses on that are absolutely pertinent for you to know.

Unity in the Body

It's so easy to observe the minutiae of interpersonal friction, that we are on the receiving end of, through the lens of rejection, suspicion, judgement and any other humanistic explanation we give such occurrences. Rather than what it usually is, an attack of the enemy on the unity of the body. It's our individualistic perception that encourages us to make assumptions about another individual. But time and again, God would want us to see that we don't war against flesh and blood, but principalities. Our battle isn't with each other. As believers, the reality is that there shouldn't be many circumstances that are unable to be reconciled. In light of the reconciliation we receive, we are implored to follow Jesus in reconciling with others. And the ultimate goal of the enemy is to cause enough cracks in the porcelain vase that it can't be repaired. Enough cracks, and the water in the vase will pour out, and not in the good Holy-Spirit-pour-out kind of way. Unity is precious in the Kingdom. What can we not overcome, if we are united? Unfortunately, most will agree with me, until that unity requires a personal cost. Whether that cost be an opinion, a method, or a hurt. However, what we do when the stakes are high, when we don't agree, when we are hurt, tells you much more about unity than when you agree. Because unity is not about conformity. Having unity when you all speak the same language, is easy. The Tower of Babel is evidence of that. But unity when we don't see eye to eye, or we don't speak the same language, that's hard work requiring intentionality.

Now, here is the risk with talking about unity; you walk away thinking that suppression, overlooking, silence and peace-keeping is unity. And you'd be wrong. Unity should never be used as a case in point for poor behaviour. The pursuit of real unity will promote the opposite reaction. Unity encourages us to walk toward resolving conflicts, opening doors of communication and transparency. It's called peace-MAKING. One of the most significant lessons I learnt through the Arrow Programme, is how to deal with conflict. The facilitator of the session said something that lit up my mind. He said, "Imagine if we were leading the way in society, on how to deal with conflict?" His vision was to be the ones whom the world consults when trying to understand how to manage conflict. Unfortunately, it's often the opposite that is true.

As a promising leader, I urge you to step back from any and every conflict and consider the enemy's agenda in such a matter, because you can be sure that he has one. Nine times out of ten, it's to create discord. It's not to actually change the sound levels, or the intricacies of the service…He doesn't really care about your service. On the other hand, God's agenda in a conflict is to arrive at greater unity, freedom and success. Because not all conflict is negative. Jesus says 'blessed are the peacemakers'.

Peacemakers, by the terminology alone, implies that there is peace to be made which would suggest that there are situations in which the making of peace is necessary. He intends for us all to be the kind of people who are active in bringing more peace into the world which may require us to face conflict. So here are the ways, I've seen how the enemy creates disunity:

- **Poorly managed conflict**
  What an opportunity for the enemy. It is critical to learn about conflict, your conflict style and how to manage it well. When we learn how to manage conflict well, we mitigate the risk of conflict turning into fights.

- **Offence**
  Yep, it's inevitable that this will happen. It's more about getting and giving people the tools to deal with it. I don't love that churches harp on about offence, but largely expect people to suppress it, or simply fail to equip them on how to get over it. Matthew 5:23-24 *"So if you are offering your gift at the altar and there remember that your brother has something against you, leave your gift there before the altar and go. First be reconciled to your brother, and then come and offer your gift"*(ESV). This verse is not talking about whether you have offended someone. It refers to those who have something against you. It actually encourages the offended party to go to the person and reconcile. That's not really how I've seen it work in churches. Our culture tends to be quite conflict avoidant. We also aren't great at receiving feedback that another has been offended. So, I guess, as a society we need more growth in this area.

- **Unforgiveness**
  This one is a no brainer, but it's pretty shocking how often Christians will say that they won't forgive, when Jesus is so direct about it. Of course, forgiveness isn't easy. I think sometimes we confuse the feeling of anger with unforgiveness.

I think you can forgive someone, and still be angry about the situation and circumstances. Forgiveness is more about what you are expecting of the other person. Are you still putting them on trial for their actions? Are you still wanting revenge or wanting them to pay? That's the unforgiveness bit. When you forgive them, you are wiping the debt clean. But you might still feel pain, upset and anger about the circumstances that you find yourself in as a result of the situation. I find that if you've forgiven someone, it's best to direct the residual pain and anguish to God and deal with it, with Him. He can handle it.

- **Misunderstanding**

There are so many misunderstandings that literally happen every day. The problem is that we often make judgements about the person and their intentions based on these misunderstandings, all the while we may never talk to them about it. This is how open communication really helps stop some conflict from getting out of hand.

- **Preferential treatment**

I recently read an article implying that favouritism is unavoidable. Yeah, I guess that is true. You will inevitably spend more time with some leaders, and less with others. You are obviously in more meetings with some colleagues than others. So, it's probably a fair statement. However, I think there is a difference between deliberate and accidental favouritism. And James talks all about this in chapter two. He gives an example of preferring the rich over the poor, and goes as far to suggest it as evil. If you make a beeline for the new person who drives into the carpark with a Mercedes, then I would call that deliberate favouritism. If you walk away from the difficult person, then it's probably deliberate. As Pastors we are supposed to treat people equally. In a big church it's next to impossible to be equal to all people, in all ways. For this reason, I am intentional about being consistent in the four following areas where favouritism can most often be observed.

- **How I greet them.**
  I greet people with the intention of showing them that I am happy to see them. Thankfully, I generally am happy to see most people.

- **How I listen to them.**
  Every person is worthy of my attention. That's just about respecting people and their voice

- **Seeing their potential.**
  I will often be asking God, and trying to see for myself, the giftings and good of a person. One of the most common questions I ask, particularly of young people is, "What do you want to do with your life?" or "What makes your heart light up?". I love watching people's faces as they describe their dreams. I remember what they say, and will often look for ways for them to express that. I've learnt enough about spiritual giftings to identify them, when someone is talking. And if I don't pick up on it, I will ask a person what they think their spiritual gift is.

☐ **Giving opportunities**
When I was coordinating creative items, I made sure that I wasn't only looking at those individuals that were obvious choices. I would pride myself on being able to identify the typically unseen performer who hadn't been given a chance to actualise their potential. Even if they weren't at their peak, I would develop them. We've all had people who have called out something in us, that we didn't see. To only select the obvious person, who usually gets chosen for everything already, doesn't help the rest of the team grow and frankly isn't great for team morale.

We also tend to forget that sometimes a person's potential rises to the new opportunity. They just need someone to believe in them. People need opportunities to grow. They aren't always aware of their capability, until they are in the new situation.

Additionally, it's often in giving opportunities that you might see the subconscious indirect biases you have. It's important to see those biases, because they affect unity and discipleship. Real servanthood disregards age, colour, race, marital status, education and gender. If we are committed to serving the body, we will be aware of our preferences that affect our choices. When I found myself selecting the same people, it would be a sign to me that I needed to get to know others. And I built a team who were as interested in identifying good people that we could develop, as much as me.

I certainly wasn't perfect in my application of these four areas, but I was committed to being as consistent as I could.

☐ Lack of communication

I often think the best reason for good everyday communication is because in the absence of it people begin to make assumptions. Those assumptions are usually inaccurate. There may be an assumption about me and my nature, or an assumption about their nature that has caused the lack of communication. I know we can't be perfect in our communication, but I would rather proactively communicate than to let them make assumptions that degrade trust. People who are close to me know that because I am a highly visual person, I am often very distractible. It's not because I am not engaged in the conversation. I just see lights, or a squirrel and my eyes follow. Because of this, I will often proactively communicate "Sorry, I am listening to you there was just something really strange on that wall". I do it, so that they don't have to doubt me. Now you might not be able to be that paranoid, my point is to say that lack of communication causes doubt and mistrust. Close the gap as often as you can, to protect unity and cohesion.

At the heart of disunity, is selfishness and individualism. A person prioritises themselves at the expense of the team. That doesn't mean that their complaints or hurt is not valid. It just means that they have prioritised that at the EXPENSE of others. It also doesn't mean that we shouldn't prioritise ourselves. It just means that your hurt or complaint can become your justification for damage. Maybe a person has carelessly aggressed on vulnerable people. Maybe the person has gossiped and slandered the name of other believers. It's not that you aren't valid for feeling a certain way, it's just that you still have to handle it appropriately. Pain and hurt doesn't give you a licence to act brashly. I mean you can, but it may cause disunity. So, some of you might be feeling pretty condemned right now. I want you to know that I've definitely been brash and said stupid things. God still forgives you. I had to own it, and I am committed to being a better leader who promotes unity. These days I ask myself "Will I be proud of my actions, if I were to reflect on them in the future?" That's how I determine my actions.

Unity in your family

If the enemy can get a husband and wife on an alternate vision, he can cause them to walk in alternate directions. And that's where it starts. Vision. Every spouse has a vision for their life. Every spouse has a vision for their marriage. They are often unstated, and they can change. But the enemy can use ministry as a way to divide and conquer. It can be that one of the spouses doesn't feel called to ministry, but feels an expectation to be a part of it. It can happen through the reduced time together. Either way, the enemy intends to break unity in a family. A husband and wife can deal with almost anything, if they are united. They can overcome the difficulties of parenting, finances, and even temptation, when they are united.

In my first year of ministry, my husband's workload exploded. His company landed this really big contract, and the workload tripled overnight. At the same time, we decided to buy a new home. So, we were ridiculously busy. We fought a lot during this period. And we ended up doing a marriage course at the end of that year, because homelife started to become quite unhealthy. The core issue was that we were both heading in different directions. We were both expecting each other to compensate for the other. I was expecting him to compensate for my new ministry role and its various demands. And he was expecting me to compensate for his work demands. Oftentimes in a family, the priority will get placed on the job that contributes the most money. Other times, the family will prioritise the person's job that has the 'ministry call' because it's seen as more important. I don't have a lot of advice to give about marriage, but I certainly would caution against elevating one partner's job over the other. My husband is equally called to his role, as I am. I have no right to assume that my job is a priority because what I am doing 'appears' more spiritual. God has called both of us to be faithful and serve. That's a general call for all believers. We are to be a blessing to our employers.

If you want expert advice on marriage, it would be best to consult the many available resources. One more word of caution; just make sure ministry doesn't become an escapism from dealing with family and marital matters. That never helps and it happens so often. I did that. And I discovered that when ministry absolutely disappointed me…it was my husband who was there, staying strong and faithful, keeping us all together. Your spouse is the only one who will be there when your ministry ends, and your children move out. So, cherish them and prioritise having a healthy marriage. Our marriages are a ministry too. I know in my case, my relatives are watching way more intently as to how my husband and I treat each other, than how big my ministry is. You'll be surprised how many people are doing the same. They may like your messages, but if they don't like how you treat your husband or wife their ears will start to close to your messages.

For the singles, your family is equally as important as the marrieds. My story at the start of this book pertaining to my parents, is testimony of that. You are still to honour your parents. You are still a witness to your family even if they are believers. God loves families - not just the family you will create in the future, but the family you are already a member of. Society makes that distinction, but God doesn't. 1 Timothy 5:8 has this startling verse: *"Anyone who does not provide for their relatives, and especially for their own household, has denied the faith and is worse than an unbeliever."* I'm sure the context would shed some light to the extremity of the statement. But at the very least we can conclude from this verse that God cares very much about how you treat your family. Which means don't abandon them for the sake of ministry giving them the dregs of your time, like I once did. They are a part of your ministry call, not just the people you lead. This tendency to compartmentalise, doesn't really appear to be consistent with scripture. Which means who you are at church, should be the same as who you are with your family and friends. So, if you love people, then love all people not just those you have a 'responsibility' over.

Personal attack

The enemy will primarily attack your relationship with God, through temptation, during times of spiritual dryness, or even the way you engage with spiritual disciplines. He may also try to detract from a real relationship by tempting you to become preoccupied with religion or legalistic behaviours. These are really ongoing matters for every believer and temptations that are not necessarily unique for those in ministry roles. But here are some of the specific types

THE ENEMY WILL ATTACK YOU

of attacks that I've observed the enemy do to those in ministry:

- **The element of surprise**
    The enemy loves to catch you off guard. I can't even tell you the number of times that I got sideswiped by something I wasn't prepared for. A comment, a meeting, a text, an email...Sometimes the situation themselves could be logically worked through, but the heightened emotion that is unnecessarily provoked by an ambush changes the nature of the circumstance altogether. All of a sudden shock kicks in, and you are left to pull yourself together instead of focusing on a suitable resolution or response. We could argue that surprises aren't necessarily an 'enemy' trait, but I would say that the resultant subjugation is totally his style. He wants you to feel on the back foot. He wants you to feel powerless, which is actually his position, and we are rather quite powerful. So be careful when a surprise attack occurs. You don't necessarily have to respond straight away. Be prepared with a standard response that buys you some time to regather yourself after the shock, and then respond. And I would question your intentions if you are the one doing the 'surprise' meetings, texts and phone calls too. When we respect each other and give benefit of the doubt, we want people to come prepared to bring a solution that benefits all. We don't want to attack at all...it's not really God's way of dealing with us.

> We underestimate the power of unity

- **Isolation or separation**
  We've covered this thoroughly in previous chapters, but certainly it's worth the reminder. The enemy wants us all to feel alone. He definitely wants you to feel alone in ministry. In my experience there are two experiences that cause people to make choices that they otherwise would not have considered. Pain and loneliness are very influential emotions. If you want to see someone in a desperate place, talk to someone who is lonely. Loneliness for sure contributes to people's propensity to sin. Loneliness has been shown to have links with porn addiction. By the way, loneliness is not about whether you have people around you, although it can be experienced that way too. It's internal. It's feeling alone in your experience. It can be related to being misunderstood or not feeling heard. So, take care to resist the enemy's suggestions that you are alone, that no one understands you, and that your experiences are unique. When you believe that lie, you'll stop trying to find those companions who can journey alongside you and show you that you definitely aren't alone.

- **Rejection and not fitting in**
  One of the easiest areas for the enemy to attack, is your sense of belonging. It is human nature to want to belong, and we all get pretty paranoid if we think that we don't fit in. The fact is, you may be able to handle the rejection of some people who you don't care a lot about. But what about those people who you respect? Those people who you wish you could learn from? Being rejected by them, can be devastating. In fact, it can make you feel like you don't fit in. And not fitting

in, certainly can make you wonder whether you are meant to be doing what you are doing. When I first started in ministry, I was so amazed at how interconnected the Christian world is. A lot of the pastors I worked with, knew so many people and had grown up with each other. I would often watch as they would be given opportunities because of the existing relationship they had. As someone who hadn't really grown up in church, this made me feel so excluded. I would often remark to God, that I was disadvantaged by not having grown up in a Christian family. I wondered sometimes why Christians wanted to make more first-generation Christians, when they made them feel like outsiders. It wasn't until I said "God, I am going to believe that you will never allow me to be disadvantaged, because of not growing up in a Christian home" that I saw how little it mattered. And He has shown me time and again, that, what looks like a disadvantage on the surface has often been an advantage. So, if you don't feel like you fit in, or that you have been rejected, just keep in mind that it doesn't mean you aren't where you are supposed to be. It may just mean that God wants you to focus on pleasing him and disregard the opinions of those around you.

Fear attacks

The enemy obviously uses fear a lot. To restrict us, and distract us. But sometimes he just does stuff to get your attention. To remind you that he is around, and to get you to cower at his presence. He only does this because he actually doesn't have power, and he doesn't want you to know that. Luke 10:19 assures us that we are the ones with the power, as a result of Christ's presence in our lives. Regardless of what he throws at you *"nothing will harm you"*. The devil may be able to encourage others to hurt us, but he himself is unable to directly cause us harm. A couple of years ago, I was driving to an appointment with a Connect Group Leader. All of a sudden an old lady pulled out of a driveway without looking. I swerved just in time to have the front side of my car hit the passenger door of her car. She sustained an injury to her leg, and the ambulance was called. But I was fine, except for a bit of shock really. If I didn't swerve exactly the way I did, who knows what would have happened? As far as I could see, there was absolutely no meaning for the accident. And the average person would have walked away thinking that these kinds of incidents are just a casualty of life. But I disagree. I knew I was protected that day. The whole experience certainly reminded me that the enemy is out to get me. Even though it's not always likely to change anything, the enemy likes to threaten us. So, if you have any attacks, which are way more common that people care to admit, just remember he is trying to get you. Whilst we don't want to be obsessed with his attacks, we also don't want to be oblivious. I'm not exactly sure how you reach that healthy medium, but at the very least be aware.

Unity may just be the most valuable endeavour

Unity is the one area that the enemy zeroes in on the most. We actually underestimate the power of unity, but he doesn't. Jesus himself in John 17:21, when praying for future believers, first asks for ONENESS. Oneness with each other, oneness with Jesus and

THE ENEMY WILL ATTACK YOU

oneness with the Father. It's the first request He makes! Just think how ridiculously staggering that fact is. Think of all the subjects He didn't pray for first. He didn't pray for revival. He didn't pray for power. He didn't pray for deliverance. He didn't pray for the lost... And He doesn't stop there, He continues to describe His vision of *'being brought to complete unity'*. It's simply incredible how we can get lost in the mechanics of church, and forget that unity is so important to Jesus. If we are truly surrendered to His headship over the body, we will recognise that unity is at the centre of His mission on earth. We understand why, right? Unity is beautiful, unity is powerful. Unity is unstoppable. When you have a team, who are on the same page, and they become skilled at leveraging each other's strengths and minimising each other's weaknesses through collaboration and understanding...and they love and show grace to each other...it's like a raging stream. If you dare to step into that stream, you will find yourself defenceless against its momentum. The only choice you have is to go with it, or fight and lose. Unity is also incredibly attractive! It's more popular than love and romance, even competing with sex. Have a think about all the most popular TV shows. The Big Bang, Seinfeld, Friends, Brooklyn 99, The Simpsons, The Office, Cheers, and Scrubs. All of these programs focus on a group of friends who care for one another. Yes, they are funny. But there is more to it than that. As a group of friends, they belong. They are unified. There are multitudes of people out there today who are sitting and watching TV programs that display friendship, belonging and unity. Something that they desire in their own life. And we as believers have the keys to this kind of reality. It comes at a cost. Usually yourself. But it is what we all desire. We all long to belong. Possibly more than any other desire. The world is watching us, when it comes to how we love each other. Jesus promises it in John 13:35, "*Your love for one another will prove to the world that you are my disciples*"(NLT). And unity, is the greatest expression of love. If I am willing to sacrifice for the sake of others, there is no greater exemplification of Christ's love in me.

Victims and unity

I have noticed this recurring theme when it comes to disunity. Often the individuals who perpetrate acts against unity, think they are justified. They often have been on the receiving end of some real or perceived mistreatment, and they have come to identify with the victim role. A victim mentality. I can understand why it happens, because when you have actually been a victim, the feelings of victimisation don't necessarily leave because the incident is over. But for believers, we aren't really 'victims', well not anymore. Not exactly. We are overcomers, and we are survivors. The life circumstances that cause pain and trauma are real, but we also have a very real hope to overcome it. Coming to a place where you can be free of that mentality, is pertinent to your journey as a believer. It's attractive to feel like the victim, because it can allow you to relegate the choices you make. Instead of recognising that we are all equally responsible for our choices, regardless of the cause. The reason the victim mentality is so detrimental to unity, is because you can feel absolutely justified in slandering, dividing, gossiping, actively seeking the removal of a co-worker, and taking no responsibility for the ways in which your actions destroy the

> Unity is the **greatest** expression of love

church and its people. Even if you have been spiritually abused, you are still responsible for your choices. That is why I think it is imperative to get treatment and deal with it. Will there be grace? Of course. But I find grace, or at least patience, can begin to waver for someone who is being destructive, whilst also refusing to get help. I've often seen consequences applied to those with a victim mentality, because really those in authority have limited options with a person who thinks everyone else is at fault and are unwilling to participate in a restorative journey. Unfortunately, even the decisions are seen through a 'victim-lens'. Those individuals are often trapped for too long, in a world created by the victim mentality that once saved them...and is now destroying them. If you have a victim mentality, do all you can to be relieved of it. And definitely heal around trusted friends who can handle hearing the pain come from your mouth. Friends who can listen and understand and not take second hand offence, are rare, but are an asset to you in ministry. I have them, and I cherish them.

Where to from here?

This chapter is unlike the other chapters, just because of its unique focus. I don't have any signs and symptoms. So here are a list of suggestions:

- **Do absolutely all you can to focus on unity**
  Remind yourself as often as you can, that unity is absolutely the most important thing. Because if it's not something you've had to think about a lot in your life, there is a good chance you will forget. Get a conviction, pray for a conviction in your heart of God's ideas about unity. Watch videos, read books and

reread books. Just do whatever you can to make sure that unity is at the front and centre of your mind when you walk into church and the church office each week. See how God thinks and speaks collectively, because much of the Bible is a collective conversation. Remember that there are no enemies in the kingdom, God wants us all to be on the same side.

☐ **Be careful when you get hurt or are hurting**
If there was ever a reason to be kind to yourself, it's because when you've had a significant blow, you probably aren't going to have the soundest perspective. Until you are able to heal and have better perspective, it's really hard to make decisions that aren't influenced by how you are feeling at the time. So maybe don't send that angry email when you know you are hurting. Maybe consider that your perception can't be trusted. When you think it would be OK to react to a comment, it's possible that your heart is deceiving itself into thinking that your emotions are correct and honest. It's amazing to me how we as a society can be so distrustful of so much, but we believe our emotions 100%. So be careful of your default solutions, when you are hurt. Give yourself time to process if needed. And introverts, just be aware that you will require a different kind of processing. Don't feel like you have to talk if you don't want to.

☐ **Engage in spiritual warfare**
Whether you participate or not, you are engaged in spiritual warfare. So, wouldn't it make more sense to engage in it, than to pretend it's not happening? When you know that you are in

the middle of a battle, where you are a secondary focus, the best you can do is pray and find Bible verses that represent the truth in your circumstances. At a time when I knew I was being slandered, I realised that there was much more going on around me and that my situation was just one of the smaller battles being fought. So, I kept my head down. I found verses that I knew spoke to my specific situation. I had them in my phone, and at my desk. I looked at them frequently. I prayed. I read. I kept my heart and mind focused on the goal. Later, God showed me how my choices had made a significant difference. Much of the battle was over, and the specific slander aimed at me had subsided with no real impact on my future. There are times, when you have to close your mouth and realise that you don't war against flesh and blood. There are probably more circumstances like that than you realised. Resist the temptation to take matters personally, just focus on the battle in the spiritual realm.

- **Ask God for a timeframe**
When life has become really difficult, I ask God for a timeframe. He often gives me a dream that would mark some kind of event on a calendar. For example, one year it was Halloween, and that was my way of knowing that something would happen by that time frame. In a particular year, I told God, instead of asking. Even if you don't hear from God, have confidence that He hears you. I would say something along the lines of, "God if nothing really changes and I can't see this one specific issue resolved, I will assume that my time here is done by the end of the year." In most cases, He would answer me. And if not,

I was prepared to make the choice. But sometimes having a timeframe gives you the strength to muster for a season. We often can keep ourselves going in intense pressure for a certain timeframe, not without consequences of course. It's when we have no idea how long it's going to last that really scares us. So, ask. It's not going to hurt.

- **Resist - stay still**
When ministry and life are really explosive, sometimes the best course of action is to do and say nothing, and simply stand firm. Jesus didn't really say a lot after he was arrested. When he was being questioned, accused, mocked and slandered, there were only a few times when he responded. We could certainly learn a lot from His response. There are times, maybe in the face of accusation and criticism that we should just not respond. I have this policy, if I can surmise from the specific situation this person has already made their mind up about a situation or me, I do not try to change their opinion. It's partly an exercise in being confident in yourself, partly an exercise in trusting God that their opinion isn't critical, partly an exercise in trusting that God will vindicate me. I try not to fight those battles, because a lot of the time they aren't really listening to you anymore either. If we are confident that we have done the right thing, or that we have adequately repented and attempted to reconcile, you can stand tall and resist the temptation to justify or explain yourself. The number of times I have to tell people: "You don't have to explain yourself to me" is quite staggering. I am not your judge, and you are not mine. So, just stand still and resist the enemy's ploys to engage in

dialogue that doesn't build better relationships. This solution of resisting and staying still, is part of why I sat in my green chair through suicidal thoughts. Sometimes we think we need these massive answers to resolve temptation. But the Bible says we are just to resist the devil, and he will flee from you. I'm not 100% sure what that looks like in a practical sense. I presumed it means doing nothing or not reacting, but there's clearly wisdom in making the enemy flee rather than trying to fix a situation yourself.

The enemy will play on your weaknesses in ministry. If you are judgemental, it will be exposed. If you are self-conscious, it will be tested. It's simply because the level of exposure required in ministry, brings it all to the surface. Unfortunately, many a leader's reaction to such exposure out of fear and vulnerability is to hide. The downside is that it's impossible to hide the 'weak' parts of you, without hiding some of the good parts as well. It's part of being a wholistic, non-compartmentalised person. The fact is, that as you become less self-conscious and more other conscious, you realise that your weaknesses aren't intended to bring you shame. We set a much greater example for others when we demonstrate an acknowledgement of weaknesses without allowing it to limit us. I wouldn't call myself the most domesticated person in the world. I will often be stacking dishes in the dishwasher and I think about this: we weren't ever meant to do life alone. Imagine if we all lived together in one big house, we would be able to leverage the strengths of each person. Which means, I might not have to do as many dishes. That's usually the agenda behind it! Recognising our weaknesses are an opportunity to engage others in the mission and allow their strengths to be released, or to enlist other options. So, don't buy into the enemy's game. You don't have to be ashamed of your weaknesses. You can take the one action he would hate most...unite with your brothers and sisters in Christ and work as a team.

The Jesus factor

So, the enemy clearly attacked Jesus and the disciples. And he definitely attacked unity. Jesus' crew had the biggest case of attack on unity that the world has ever seen. Judas. A man who actually walked with Jesus for three years, but sold him out to a torturous death. It is so significant that Jesus death was caused by a betrayal of someone within his own ranks. But it doesn't end there. There's the time that the disciples began arguing over who was the greatest. There's the rather annoying competition between John, the disciple Jesus loved, and Peter. And then of course, Peter denies Jesus three times. There were plenty of opportunities for disunity to have wreaked havoc in the team. But I guess that's kind of the point. Even the group that literally had the Messiah in its midst, could fall so easily into the grips of disunity. But Jesus is perfect in his dealings with the disciples. He confronts when necessary, He gives grace, He demonstrates unconditional love. He doesn't treat Judas differently in spite of knowing that He will betray Him. He doesn't make a big deal about Peter's denial, He gives Him a second chance. He is quick to resolve any matters that could harm the unity of His leaders. As demonstrated earlier, unity is important to God. Sometimes we have to war for it, but ALWAYS we are called to demonstrate it. As leaders, we should think about it, because often many aren't.

THE ENEMY WILL ATTACK YOU

We can't control the environment, but we can make some clear boundaries about unifying and un-unifying behaviours. Hebrews 12:14 reminds us to *"Strive for peace with everyone"* (ESV). This is a call for every believer. Let's learn how to do that, so that our people learn how important it is to God too.

Conclusion

When I was in my 20's, there is a moment that will be forever etched in my memory. I was getting ready and talking to God. I told Him that I wanted Him to use my life as a message to His people or the world. That I would surrender my future and story, for His glory. And I meant it.

See, I had been reading about Hosea. Rather than just preach at God's people, Hosea was called to have his life be a message. God asks him to marry a known adulterer and he obeys. Imagine that? Imagine knowing that you are going to marry someone who is not going to be faithful to you? Imagine how foolish you would look to those around you? We would struggle in this day and age to be this surrendered. Well, I was praying this prayer, because I was telling God that I was willing to look foolish for Him. That I was willing to obey Him, regardless of how ridiculous the request was.

I do believe, that God has answered that request on more occasions than I can recall. Yay for me! Church leadership is just one of those areas. I believe that my ministry story brings glory to Him. But I also believe that my ministry story is His message to any leader who cares to listen to the warning's and encouragement. I hope that in my efforts, that inevitably looked foolish, you can see God's message to you.

CONCLUSION

Ministry is hard. I've said it several times already. Maybe it's too hard! Certainly, all the areas I have reflected on in this book, may have caused you to wonder at times why anyone would invest their life in ministry. We do it because we are called. But that doesn't mean that ministry should stay the way it is. The way it's being practiced today, isn't necessarily the way it must be done. It's just how it has become. Of course, there are non-negotiables. But not every method we use in ministry is steeped in biblical principles. It's possible that there is a better way for it to be done that might make church leadership more accessible and sustaining. Here are some thoughts I have about that:

- **Stop the secrecy, share more openly**
  I'm not by any means an expert at the stuff I've shared in this book. They are simply my observations. I'm OK with being wrong, if it means creating dialogue. Part of my honesty in this book is an effort to open the communication. I figure that if I can share, so can you. I think we make ministry harder when we are insistent on going it alone. Opening the communication lines doesn't mean slander or gossip either. I'm not talking about airing your specific frustrations with your church and co-workers, that would bring disrepute and disunity. It is really important for you to have a friend that you can talk to about those frustrations, but please: chose one person, who is out of your context, who you know you can trust and won't judge you. Also pick someone who will challenge you. But the life challenges, the disappointments… those are aspects that we should be real about with each other. The secrecy has made ministry pretty difficult to endure. When we are real, we let the walls down for everyone.

- **Get better at supporting each other against the enemy**
  So, I'm not big-noting myself, but the actual functions of being a pastor weren't really that hard for me. I was doing way harder tasks, with bigger organisations in my previous employment: talking to hurting people, negotiating, writing strategies and implementing programs. They aren't the areas that I struggled with in ministry. The biggest struggle for me was seeing how Christians treat each other. If they always acted with humility, it probably wouldn't bother me. But often they are just stubborn and proud, whilst they gossip, slander and attack. Unfortunately, I received some 'slander'. And at times I was treated like I was the enemy. It wasn't fun. Those were the occurrences that really dragged me down. But how much better would it be, if instead of jumping to conclusions about each other, we gave the benefit of the doubt. If we could just look for the ways the enemy is working, instead of simply pointing the finger at each other, we would go a long way to supporting each other.

- **Be less of a business sometimes, and more of a body of believers**
  I certainly have a tendency to be business-like in certain ways. I prefer when workplaces are professional, and there is a certain level of professional courtesy I expected working at the church too. But, there are times when we ought to recognise that we are a church firstly and an organisation secondly. There are times when we should drop the boss-employee role, and the staff-congregation role, and just be brothers and sisters in Christ. Walk alongside each other as

equals, rather than the official capacities we create. I have this dream, that one day I am in a role where I am allowed to do something like what I am about to describe: I imagine that we hold an evening service, in the early parts of the year, where all the staff, their spouses and families are brought together. At this gathering, we would pray individually for every child of a staff member, and give them an encouraging word, vision, prophecy, a verse or whatever God gives to us. To speak into their future. Then we would pray for the spouses. We would bless them, give them a verse and speak into their lives. This vision moves my heart every time. Imagine if we believed we were 'on a mission' together, instead of seeing ourselves in an organisational, functional, transactional relationship. I have always offered myself as a coach or mentor to kids of staff, and I will never stop doing that. Far too often, it doesn't feel like their church because of their parent's roles. I want my daughter and every child of a staff member to feel like their church is their home, instead of mum or dads 'work'. Maybe it's not possible, but I won't stop dreaming it. Such things fuel my passion.

Co-shepherding?

In organisational psychology there is a concept called role ambiguity. This is the degree to which a worker is unclear of expectations, responsibilities and authority in their role. Role ambiguity can be considered significant in the worker's experience and success. Role ambiguity can happen a number of ways, and the role of a supervisor is very significant. In fact, it often has a direct impact on the reported levels of job satisfaction. I presume that some of you are already trying to connect dots, and think that I may be suggesting that role ambiguity is an issue in churches. Yes, I think it would be the case for some churches. My bigger concern is that I don't know if we fully understand our roles as God sees it. I don't actually have the answer by the way, I am more wanting to point out my own confusion. The number of times I have been reminded that I am a shepherd is too many to count. So, I just assumed that my role was a shepherd, with little questioning. And many of you wouldn't disagree. However, in Ezekiel 34, God is relaying with vigour that He will remove the shepherds of Israel and He will be the Shepherd of His people, because the existing shepherds had done such a poor job. Later in John 10, Jesus is calling Himself the 'Good Shepherd'. I understand that this is to fulfil the prophecy as noted in Ezekiel 34. My question is, how can Jesus and I simultaneously be shepherd's?

Surely this would make us co-shepherds, right? Our role as shepherds, is secondary to Jesus' role as the shepherd. So that would make us co-shepherds. That may not seem like such a significant distinction. But consider this, if you were told you were the boss of a company, and that another person had also been appointed as the boss, what would be your biggest concern? Assume that your position descriptions were exactly the same, and your performance indicators. My biggest concern, if I were to entertain the idea, would be figuring out what distinguishes my role from theirs. How would our tasks differ, so that we weren't doubling up? We would also have to figure out how we make decisions together, and where the

CONCLUSION

authority starts and ends. It would then take time to determine the workstyle, preferences, strengths and weaknesses, so as to leverage and enhance a positive working relationship. For it to work, it would have to be the most collaborative work setups you could have, and for that reason also fraught with risk. My point is, it's not simple. It's highly complex. Not impossible of course, but just a lot of effort to maintain, with great rewards if done well. So, if we are co-shepherds, which it seems to be, what does scripture say about the role we are meant to play and the role He is meant to play in building the Kingdom? Because it wouldn't be the same. It is simply beautiful to me, to consider that Jesus has instigated a situation in which seamless collaboration is intended to reside. It would be so like Him to do that. But I feel like there is some unstated role ambiguity between Jesus as the shepherd, and us as co-shepherds. And if we are co-shepherds, when am I stepping on Jesus' toes? What part is His, and what part is mine? What authority do I have, if any? I could probably spend a lot of time trying to understand it myself by searching through scripture, but alas, I have reached the end of my expertise. But maybe the reason why ministry is so hard, is because we've been trying to take responsibility, for that which we were never supposed to. I don't know. I realise I am thinking quite conceptually here and maybe it makes no difference practically. But with the havoc that has been heaped on the lives of pastors on account of the weight of ministry, maybe we should be asking whether we have had it wrong all along. Maybe this co-shepherd distinction holds the answer. So, if someone out there who is more theologically sound then me wants to research it, please do. You may hold the answers to a significant change that we've all been desperately wanting.

So, it seems as though we have now reached the end of my ramblings. I know many won't like the matters I have raised, but I have shared openly for you the reader, because my heart is deep with compassion for those that labour for Christ. But here are my absolute final thoughts. My heart's desire is that you deepen your love for God. That you sustain yourself in ministry. That when the time comes to leave, you are led out in peace and joy. Be like Christ on all occasions, don't just preach Him on Sundays. Be a disciple first, and a leader second. Stay humble, steward power well. You are here because He wills it, you didn't earn it. Beware the bubble, and refrain from seeking validation in ministry. Be quick to seek help in your hard times. Maintain a healthy perspective, and never forget your family. And this:

> *"Jesus called them together and said, "You know that the rulers of the Gentiles lord it over them, and their high officials exercise authority over them. Not so with you. Instead, whoever wants to become great among you must be your servant, and whoever wants to be first must be your slave- just as the Son of Man did not come to be served, but to serve, and to give his life as a ransom for many." Matthew 20:25-28*

Blessings

Melanie J. Saward
melj.saward@gmail.com

Reference List

Introduction

1. The Arrow Emerging Leaders program is a two year program that focuses on developing emerging leaders in church, parachurch and missional movements. To find out more visit www.arrowleadership.org.au.

Chapter 2

2. Nieuwhof, C. (2019). 5 Disruptive Church Trends That Will Rule 2019. [Blog] *Carey Nieuwhof.* Available at: https://careynieuwhof.com/5-disruptive-church-trends-that-will-rule-2019/ [Accessed 20 Jan. 2019].

3. Keller, T. (2011). *Counterfeit gods.* New York: Riverhead Books.

4. *The Founder.* (2016). [film] Directed by J. Hancock. Douglasville, Georgia: FilmNation Entertainment.

5. *Fyre: The Greatest Party That Never Happened.* (2019). [film] Directed by C. Smith. United States: Jerry Media, Vice Studios & Library Films.

6. Timothy J. Legg, C. (2019). *Impostor syndrome: Symptoms, types, and how to deal with it.* [online] Medical News Today. Available at: https://www.medicalnewstoday.com/articles/321730.php [Accessed 1 Feb. 2019].

Chapter 3

7. *The Nutty Professor.* (1996). [film] Directed by T. Shadyac. Beverly Hills, California: Imagine Entertainment.
8. Rainer, T. and Geiger, E. (2014). *Simple Church.* Nashville, Tennessee: B & H Publishing Group.

Chapter 4

9. Allen, D. (2001). *Getting Things Done: The Art of Stress-free Productivity.* 2nd ed. Penguin Books, p.5.
10. Walling, T. (2008). *Stuck!: Navigating The Transitions of Life & Leadership.* 2nd ed. Chico, California: Leader Breakthru.
11. Eguchi, H., Wada, K. and Smith, D. (2016). Recognition, Compensation, and Prevention of Karoshi, or Death due to Overwork. *Journal of Occupational and Environmental Medicine,* 58(8), pp.e313-e314.
12. Seinfeld "The Reverse Peephole" Season 9, Episode 12, (2019). [TV programme] NBC.

Chapter 5

13. *The Talented Mr Ripley.* (1999). [film] Directed by A. Minghella. Italy: Miramax, Paramount Pictures, Mirage Enterprises, Timnick Films.
14. Ortberg, J. (2002). *The Life You've Always Wanted: Spiritual Disciplines for Ordinary People.* 2nd ed. Grand Rapids, Michigan: Zondervan.
15. Collins, J. (2001). *Good to Great: Why Some Companies Make the Leap...and Others Don't.* London: Random House Business Books, pp.17-38.

REFERENCE LIST

16. Maxwell, J. (2002). *The 21 irrefutable laws of leadership workbook*. Nashville, Tenn.: Thomas Nelson Publishers.
17. Dean, J. (2013). *Making Habits, Breaking Habits*. Boston, Massachusetts: Da Capo Press.

Chapter 7

18. Furtick, P. (2018). *Where's Your Confidence*. [video] Available at: https://www.youtube.com/watch?v=u6CWFzhq9AA [Accessed 3 Oct. 2018].

www.ingramcontent.com/pod-product-compliance
Lightning Source LLC
Chambersburg PA
CBHW070139100426
42743CB00013B/2761